*Foundation Theology
2008*

Foundation Theology 2008

Faculty Essays for
Ministry Professionals

Edited by John H. Morgan

The Victoria Press

South Bend

BR
50
.F580
2008

JKM Library
1100 East 55th Street
Chicago, IL 60615

Foundation Theology 2008: Faculty Essays for Ministry Professionals

Edited by John H. Morgan

Copyright ©2008
All Rights Reserved

Published on behalf of the Graduate Theological Foundation by
The Victoria Press
An Imprint of Lirio Corporation
South Bend, Indiana 46601
www.TheVictoriaPress.com

Library of Congress Control Number: 2008925039
ISBN-13: 978-1-929569-52-6
ISBN-10: 1-929569-52-1

Printed in the United States of America
on recycled paper made from 100% post-consumer waste

Contents

Editor's Note   vii

Islam and the Pope   1
  Senad Agić

Holiness and Monstrosity:
  The Legend of Christopher, the Dog-Headed Saint   15
  Dennis J. Billy, C.Ss.R.

Liturgical Formation as an Agent of Transformation   27
  Robin P P Gibbons

Dying as "The Journey Home"   43
  Ann V. Graber

The Beloved Community:
  Martin Luther King, Jr. and Hope for the City   59
  C. Anthony Hunt

The Moral Responsibility of Leadership
  in Tenuous Times: A Higher Imperative   77
  Paul J. Kirbas

Animal Experiments:
   Ethics, Theology, and the Possibility of Dialogue   89
   Andrew Linzey

Pope Benedict and the Jews   101
   James R. Michaels

Religion Without God:
   Exploring the Perimeters of Huxley's Humanism   117
   John H. Morgan

Pope Benedict XVI on Islam:
   Setting the Stage for a Culture of Dialogue   131
   Bernard J. O'Connor

Espiritualidad Masculina   151
   Antonio Ramirez

The Jewish Setting of the Lord's Prayer   167
   Peter E. Roussakis

Re-imagining the Anglican Communion   179
   Vincent Strudwick

About the Contributors   *199*

Editor's Note

For nearly fifty years, the Graduate Theological Foundation has demonstrated through research, teaching, and publications its fundamental commitment to scholarship in the field of ministry education. This commitment has been based upon our belief that knowledge is a panacea for effectively addressing the problems of the world, problems which are generated by misunderstanding, miscommunication, and misinformation. In an effort to reach the broadest possible spectrum of well-intentioned communities and individuals, the Foundation has embraced a concept of ministry which is ubiquitous within the human experience.

Our definition of ministry is regularly recited as an address to the troubling issues confronting our world today. We now recite that definition again here for all to read: *Owing to the accelerated blurring of lines between the sacred and secular in contemporary society, today's professionals are continually pressed to craft a redefinition of the nature and role of their work within this matrix of convergence which takes account of both personal value-oriented service and public responsibility. The Foundation has, from its inception, chosen to define ministry both within specific faith communities and within the broader society in terms of those professionals involved in human social services in which the practitioner is self-reflectively aware of the nurturing quality of that activity. Individuals who define their professional activity as being of service to the improvement and nurture of society and the world community, including such fields as education, pastoral assignments, chaplaincy, mediation, management, media services, health care and counseling, are recognized by the Foundation as being in ministry.*

The essays collected in this monograph have been written by members of our distinguished and internationally acclaimed faculty and address issues related to the Papacy, religious humanism, animal rights, holiness and spirituality, and the Anglican Communion. The Foundation continues to maintain a firm commitment to religious scholarship and an unrelenting involvement in the nurturing of compassion and liberality within the human community.

John H. Morgan
President
Spring, 2008

In the Name of God, the Compassionate, the Merciful

Islam and the Pope
Senad Agić

*"If one takes a one life,
it is as if one has taken the life of all
humanity.*

*If one saves a single life,
it is as if he has saved the life of all
humanity."*

Qur'an 5:32

*"I have set before you life,
and I have set before you death. I
have begged you to choose life
for the sake of your children."*

Deuteronomy

We live in a very precarious time in our human history. We live in an era of globalization. And there are many ways of looking at this globalized world. The world in which we live has shrunk, it has become like a small village. Information technology has enabled us to communicate with the rest of the world like never before. We are not only witnesses of global events, but we are inevitably a part of them.

Without peace and justice between Muslims and Christians, there can be no meaningful peace in the world. The future of the world depends on cooperation and goodwill between Muslims and Christians.

Love of the One God, and love of the neighbor are principles found over and over again in the sacred texts of Islam and Christianity. The Unity of God, the necessity of love for Him, and the necessity of love for the neighbor is a common theme.

In the Holy *Qur'an*, God Most High enjoins Muslims to issue the following call to Christians (and Jews—the *People of the Scripture*):

> *Say: O People of the Scripture! Come to a common word between us and you: that we shall worship none but God, and that we shall ascribe no partner unto Him, and that none of us shall take others for lords beside God. And if they turn away, then say: Bear witness that we are they who have surrendered (unto Him).* (Aal 'Imran 3:64)

To love thy neighbor is an essential and integral part of faith in God. The well known "golden rule" is as familiar to Muslims as it is to Christians. The Prophet Muhammad, peace be upon him, said: "*None of you has faith until you love for your brother what you love for yourself.*" And: "*None of you has faith until you love for your neighbour what you love for yourself.*"

Sympathy for one's neighbor - and even formal interfaith prayers - are not enough. They must be accompanied by generosity and self-sacrifice or else as one leading Turkish scholar of inter-religious dialogue wrote, "We live in a world in which either we live together or we will perish together."[1]

God says in the Holy *Qur'an*:

> *It is not righteousness that ye turn your faces to the East and the West; but righteous is he who believeth in God and the Last Day and the angels and the Scripture and the prophets; and*

giveth wealth, for love of Him, to kinsfolk and to orphans and the needy and the wayfarer and to those who ask, and to set slaves free; and observeth proper worship and payeth the poor-due. And those who keep their treaty when they make one, and the patient in tribulation and adversity and time of stress. Such are they who are sincere. Such are the pious.

(Al-Baqarah 2:177)

And also:

Ye will not attain unto righteousness until ye expend of that which ye love. And whatsoever ye expend, God is Aware thereof.

(*Aal 'Imran*, 3:92)

Without giving our neighbors what we ourselves love, we do not truly love God or our neighbor.

Open Letters

Do you know what is better than charity and fasting and prayer? It is keeping peace and good relations between people, as quarrels and bad feelings destroy mankind.

Prophet Muhammad (PBUH)

On October 13th, 2006, one month to the day after Pope Benedict XVI's Regensburg address of September 13th, 2006, 38 Islamic authorities and scholars from around the world, representing all denominations and schools of thought, joined together to deliver an answer to the Pope in the spirit of open intellectual exchange and mutual understanding. In their *Open Letter to the Pope*, for the first time in recent history, Muslim scholars from every branch of

Islam spoke with one voice about the true teachings of Islam.

One year after that letter, Muslims have expanded their message. In *A Common Word Between Us and You*, 138 Muslim scholars, clerics and intellectuals have unanimously come together for the first time since the days of the Prophet, peace be upon him, to declare the common ground between Christianity and Islam. Like the *Open Letter*, the signatories to this message come from every denomination and school of thought in Islam. Every major Islamic country or region in the world is represented in this message, which is addressed to the leaders of all the world's churches, and indeed to all Christians everywhere.

The final form of the letter was presented at a conference in September 2007 held under the theme of "Love in the *Qur'an*," by the *Royal Academy* of *The Royal Aal al-Bayt Institute for Islamic Thought* in Jordan, under the Patronage of H.M. King Abdullah II. Indeed, the most fundamental common ground between Islam and Christianity, and the best basis for future dialogue and understanding, is the love of God and love for the neighbor that comes from loving God.

Never before have Muslims delivered this kind of definitive consensus statement on Christianity. Rather than engage in a polemic, the signatories have adopted the traditional and mainstream Islamic position of respecting the Christian scripture and calling Christians to be more, not less, faithful to it.

It is hoped that this document will provide a common constitution for the many worthy organizations and individuals who are carrying out interfaith dialogue all over the world. Often these groups are unaware of each other, and duplicate each other's efforts. Not only can *A Common Word Between Us* give them a starting point for cooperation and worldwide co-ordination, but it does so on the most solid theological ground possible: the teachings of the *Qur'an* and the Prophet, and the commandments described by Jesus Christ, peace be upon him, in the Bible. Thus, despite their differences, Islam and Christianity not only share the same

Divine Origin and the same Abrahamic heritage, but the same greatest commandments.

Open and Sincere Advice

> *Oh, Mankind! We created you from a single soul, male and female, (Adam and Eve) and made you into nations and tribes, so that you may come to know one another (not to despise each other). Truly, the most honored of you in God's sight is the one who is most righteous.* Qur'an, 49:13

Pope Benedict XVI's Regensburg address of September 13, 2006 unfortunately suggested that this Pope apparently clings to past understandings of religious relations and the stereotyping and denigration of Islam. He loses sight of the fact that Islam insists that "There is no compulsion in religion." As a consequence, the Pope functioned as a tragically divisive force in the global community. No living religious tradition should use medieval interpretations ignoring modern realities. Imagine any influential imam quoting today from Christian medieval sources the words of enmity uttered towards Islam and Muslims. Ignorance and a lack of goodwill are to be blamed as the primary reason why people with different religious beliefs and doctrines in the past often sought to challenge and even eliminate each other. When televangelist Pat Robertson, explained his support for presidential candidate Rudy Giuliani (*Wall Street Journal*, November 8, 2007), he said, "To me, the overriding issue before the American people is the defense of our population from the bloodlust of Islamic terrorists." We, the American Muslims, know that such rhetoric represents a promotion of the strategy of fear. We know that his sentiment is consistent with the Bush administration strategy, implemented after September 11, 2001, which promotes a climate of fear as a way to fight Islamic-inspired "terrorism." The image of Islam has been devastated as a result of sheer ignorance, hatred, and lack of awareness. We need now, more than ever, religious leaders who, unlike Pat Robertson and Pope Benedict XVI, can lead us beyond the politics of fear.

Islam can not be destroyed. It has been built by Allah Almighty. Creation has no power when compared to the Almighty. If all of creation were to come together, it could not do anything, and could not even remove one cubic millimeter of stone from the proverbial building of Islam. If the people of the whole world should come together and if the power of all men and all *jinn* reaches them they wouldn't be able to remove even one stone from the building of Islam because the building has been built by Allah and it belongs to Him.

"Exclusivists hold that their religion is the only truth and that no other ideas are needed to answer the question of human existence. Pluralists, on the other extreme, claim that no religion has claim to the truth and that all religions are true, just as all cultures are acceptable – a relativist position. Inclusivists take the middle ground, the position asserting that one religion is correct and true, and that other religions do have value."[2]

If history teaches us anything from today's perspective, it should teach us to respect the rights of all people, and to peacefully coexist with one another. If we want to build bridges needed to create peace and harmony then we need to form strong and altruistic, tolerant, kind and benevolent individuals and communities, break down barriers which separate us, and then rely on our common Lord.

We all must work harder to build mutual respect, an attitude of forbearance regardless of the doctrines which we may live by. If we disagree, we do so with respect and civility. We should move a step further to cultivate a spirit of affirmative gratitude for those who do not see things as we see them without compromising our theology. We should harbor not only tolerance toward one another, but also genuine goodwill.

Open Dialogue as a Way

To each among you (various groups/races - not excluding anybody) we have prescribed the Law (Torah, Gospels, Qur'an, etc.) and an Open Way (given a conscience with reference to the indigenous people). If God had willed, all humanity would have been of one single community. This is not a part of God's plan. God's plan is to test you in what each one has received (in form of Holy Scriptures or Conscience). So strive, as in a race in all virtues. The goal of all the people is to God. God (alone) will tell you the truth in matters of which you dispute. *Qur'an*, 5:48

Religion is increasingly dominant in the contemporary world. Huntington rightly stated: "In the modern world, religion is a central, perhaps the central force that motivates and mobilizes people; what ultimately counts for people is not political ideology or economic interest. Faith and family, blood and belief, are what people identify with and what they will fight and die for."[3]

If we look at the present situation in the world we will realize that many conflicts have been provoked, or invoked, by religious feelings. Without doubt religion can be misused and religious feelings manipulated. When this is done by religious leaders, religion itself is being damaged and the ideal of living together with others in a peaceful world-order is compromised. My objection here is not to suggest that religions themselves have a high potential to cause conflict threatening world peace. All of them urge their followers to do unto others what they would like to be done to themselves.

However, sometimes, in order to influence followers and to increase their self-worth, leaders have articulated their views negatively, particularly in the context of urging followers to protect themselves, their belongings, or their race, ethnicity, culture and faith. But if we are not ready to extend to others the same respect that we would wish for ourselves, no matter how much we claim to love them, we in reality do not love them. With such an attitude our dialogue will fail. Hans Küng rightly states when speaking of Samuel Huntington's thesis, the "clash of civilizations," that "Civilizations and religions have not only high potential for conflict but also a high potential for peace, which they have shown not only in the revelation in Eastern Europe but also in the removal of dictatorship in the Philippines and the abolition of Apartheid in South Africa."[4]

Al-Hamdu Lillah (Praise be to God), still the major world religions do invite their followers to love their neighbors as they love themselves. Of course, we do not love them completely unless we are ready to dialogue with them and they with us, and unless we and they are ready to promote past positive models of co-existence and develop them further to suit our time and challenges in the modern world, healing our past traumatic memories and dissolving all of our mutually hostile stereotypes and misunderstandings.

Pope John Paul II worked tirelessly to advance the cause of Christianity, to lift the burdens of stereotypes and to speak fearlessly on behalf of moral values and human dignity. He is greatly missed, particularly by those who have looked to him for leadership. May we keep building bridges of understanding and common ground instead of battle grounds, and a globalization of security that will end our mutual mistrust and bring us peace, friendship, and true goodwill toward one another.

Hans Küng's Open Challenge

> *Stand out firmly for Justice as witnesses in front of God, even against yourselves, against your children and against your parents, against people who are rich (lobbyists) or poor. Do not follow your inclinations or your desires, lest you should deviate from Justice. Remember God is the best of all Protectors and well acquainted with all that you do. Qur'an, 4:135*

Hans Küng, a Swiss Catholic theologian and prolific scholar, after a life-long study of Christianity and other faith-traditions, proposed a compelling theorem for global peace in our time of millennial change and unrest in world history.

This theorem states, "No peace among the nations without peace among the religions."[5]

Its corollary reads, "No peace among the religions without dialogue between the religions. No dialogue between the religions without investigations of the foundations of the religions."

No scholar or theologian – leaving aside the fact he happens to be Christian – has done as much in recent years in living the ideals of the above proposition as has Hans Küng. Remaining faithful to the life and teachings of Jesus Christ, Hans Küng has plunged deep in studying Hinduism, Buddhism and Confucianism.

But his most passionate commitment in this journey of reaching out has been directed towards Judaism and Islam which together with Christianity form the triangle of familial Abrahamic faith-traditions. Hence, another reading of Kung's peace theorem would be there can be no peace unless this broken triangle of the Abrahamic faith-traditions gets repaired.

Kung's devotion in getting this triangle repaired – of bringing Jews, Christians and Muslims together on the common ground of being faithful to the God of Abraham – is humbling for those who believe, irrespective of what any faith-doctrine might teach in exclusivist language, that Abraham's God is lovingly and mercifully embracing of all His children.

In this missionary task, Küng has published this year his much anticipated study simply titled *Islam: Past, Present and Future*.

Kung's *Islam* deserves the widest attention and reading. Most ironically, and urgently, it should be read by Muslims, and especially by those Muslims residing in the West most driven to apologetics and polemics with others.

There is no Muslim scholar I can readily think of who might be mentioned in the same breath as Küng for engaging with similar devotion and humility in the study of Judaism and Christianity, while putting aside any expectation that Muslims should similarly engage in studying and learning from the faith-traditions nominally described as Eastern religions.

Radicalism, bigotry and violence have left their marks, as Küng discusses, on Judaism, Christianity and Islam.

No adherent of any of these three faith-traditions can plead innocence in God's court of wrongfully spilling blood of others.

But Küng is right in asking, "Did any religion pursue a victorious course as rapid, far-reaching, tenacious and permanent as that of Islam? Scarcely one."

Küng's challenge for Muslims is remaining faithful to Abraham's God without sinking into oblivion under the weight of their history that has become mostly irrelevant, if not entirely redundant.

And Küng's challenge for others is remaining mindful of their less-than-ideal history when engaging in the urgent work of repairing the broken triangle of the Abrahamic faith-traditions.

Al Andalus "the ornament of the world."

I waste not the labor of any that labors amongst you, be they male or female, each one of you are equal to me. Qur'an, 3:195

The lessons of history, like the lessons of religion, sometime neglect examples of tolerance. Some bridge building may also be needed at home. Only two in five Americans express a favorable view of Islam. Unfavorable views are particularly strong among the elderly, political conservatives, white evangelical Protestants, Americans who live in rural areas and the South, and those who never attended college.

A thousand years ago on the Iberian Peninsula, an enlightened vision of Islam had created the most advanced culture in Europe. A nun in Saxony learned of this kingdom from a bishop, the caliph's ambassador to Germany and one of several prominent members of his diplomatic corps who were not Muslims; the bishop most likely reported to the man who ran the foreign ministry, who was a Jew.

Al Andalus, as the Muslims called their Spanish homeland, prospered in a culture of openness and assimilation. The nun, named Hroswitha, called it "the ornament of the world."

Her admiration stemmed from the cultural prosperity of the caliphate based in Cordoba, where the library housed some 400,000 volumes at a time when the largest library in Latin Christendom probably held no more than 400. What strikes us today about Al Andalus is that it was a chapter of European history during which Jews, Christians and Muslims lived side by side and, despite intractable differences and enduring hostilities, nurtured a culture of tolerance.

For many who came to know Andalusian culture throughout the Middle Ages, whether at first hand or from afar – from reading a translation produced there or from hearing a poem sung by one of its renowned singers - the bright lights of that world, and their illumination of the rest of the universe, transcended differences of religion. It was in Al Andalus that the profoundly Arabized Jews rediscovered and reinvented Hebrew poetry. Much of what was created and instilled under Muslim rule survived in Christian territories, and Christians embraced nearly all aspects of Arabic style - from philosophy to architecture. Christian palaces and churches, like Jewish synagogues, were often built in the style of the Muslims, the walls often covered with Arabic writing; one synagogue in Toledo even includes inscriptions from the Koran.

And it was throughout medieval Europe that men of unshakable faith, like Abelard and Maimonides and Averroes, saw no contradiction in pursuing the truth, whether philosophical or scientific or religious, across confessional lines. This was an approach to life - and its artistic, intellectual and religious pursuits - that was contested by many, sometimes violently, as it is today. Yet it remained a powerful force for hundreds of years.

Whether it is because of our mistaken notions about the relative backwardness of the Middle Ages or our own contemporary expectations that culture, religion and political ideology will be roughly consistent, we are likely to be taken aback by many of the lasting monuments of this Andalusian culture. The tomb of St. Ferdinand, the king remembered as the Christian conqueror of the last of all the Islamic territories, save Granada, is matter-of-factly inscribed in Arabic, Hebrew, Latin and Castilian.

The caliphate was not destroyed by Christian-Muslim warfare. It lasted for several hundred years - roughly the lifespan of the American republic to date - and its downfall was a series of terrible civil wars among Muslims.

But in the end, much of Europe far beyond the Andalusian world was shaped by the vision of complex and contradictory identities that was first made into an art form by the Andalusians. The enemies of this kind of cultural openness have always existed within each of our monotheistic religions, and often enough their visions of those faiths have triumphed. But at this time of year, and at this point in history, we should remember those moments when it was tolerance that won the day.

Notes

1 Mehmet S Aydin, *From Clashes of Civilization to Dialogue of Civilization*, Istanbul, 2000, p. 42.

2 R. Lanier Britsch, Foreword to *Religions of the World: A latter-day Saint View* by Spencer J. Palmer, Roger R. Keller, Dong Sull Choi, James A. Toronto (Provo, Utah: BYU Press, 1997), ix.

3 Samuel Huntington, "Response", p. 210, pp. 191-194, quoted from Hans Kung, *Christianity: the Religious Situation of Our Time*, London: SCM Press, p. 781.

4   Hans Küng, "Editorial: Islam-A Challenge to Christianity," Hans Küng and Jurgen Moltmann, eds., *Islam: a Challenge for Christianity*, London: Consilium (SCM), 1994/3, p. vii.

5   Salim Mansur, *Theologian finds peace path*, *Toronto Sun*, December 29, 2007.

Holiness and Monstrosity: The Legend of Christopher, the Dog-Headed Saint

Dennis J. Billy, C.Ss.R.

Soon after the close of the Second Vatican Council, a number of saints were taken off the liturgical calendar because there was little concrete historical evidence of them ever having existed. Although popular devotion to them could be deep and, at times, even widespread, the stories of their lives seemed to have much more in common with legend and myth than with verifiable historical sources. While the Church never officially denied their sainthood or actively sought to suppress their cults, its decision to remove them from the calendar relegated them to the status of second-or-third class saints.

Of those removed, probably the best known is St. Christopher, the patron saint of travelers, whose name in Greek means "Christ-bearer." Although his legend normally relates the story of a giant solitary who puts his life in peril by carrying the Christ child across a treacherous brook, it exists in a number of other versions that stir the imagination and convey important truths about the nature of Christian sanctity. One in particular presents him as a dog-headed prophet --- part man and part beast--- whose holiness and physical monstrosity highlight the shallow beauty and moral depravity of the people he is sent to convert.[1]

The Dog-Headed Saint

As the legend goes, a giant named Reprobus ("false or spurious one"), of nearly 12 cubits in height comes from an island where there lives a race of dog-headed people. Upon receiving instruction in the faith and baptism, he receives the name, Christopher ("Christ-bearer"), and is told by a voice from a cloud descending upon him from heaven that he will lead many people to the faith. After hearing these words, Christopher gives thanks to God, who can convert sinners just as easily as he can confer on wild beasts the gift of human speech. Of this, Christopher himself is living proof.

Later, Christopher enters the pagan city of Samos in Syria ruled by the evil King Dagnus. As he walks through the city, a woman on her way to pay homage to the gods sees this dog-headed giant and runs throughout the city crying out in utter bewilderment. A crowd gathers to see this monstrous sight. Standing in prayer, Christopher plants his staff in the ground and asks the Lord God to allow it to sprout flowers. God answers his prayer and, upon seeing the staff's miraculous foliage, many of the townspeople come to believe.

Upon hearing of Christopher, King Dagnus sends two large contingents of soldiers to take him prisoner and bring him to the palace. Although they are afraid of this dog-headed giant's enormous size and strange outward appearance, the king's soldiers listen to his message and convert to the Christian faith. After their conversion, Christopher accompanies them to the king of his own free will. When the king sees this dog-headed prophet, he is so taken aback that he loses his balance and falls off his chair. When asked about his designs, Christopher tells the king that he has come to the city to lead many souls to Jesus Christ, including the king himself. On hearing these remarks, the king curses Christopher and his God. He becomes further enraged when Christopher refuses to offer sacrifice to Jove and Apollo, the chief gods of the city. He orders Christopher to be thrown into prison, but the soldiers refuse to lay a hand on him. They openly reveal their newfound faith and refuse to accept the king's offer of gold and silver in return for their loyalty. Angered by their insolence, the king turns on them and orders them beheaded.

Christopher goes to prison of his own free will, without a military escort. Once the dog-headed giant is behind bars, the king seeks to tempt him by sending two prostitutes to his cell to make love to him and get him to offer sacrifice to the gods. When seeing Christopher in his cell, however, they are deeply struck by his aura of holiness and undergo a complete change of heart. They express sorrow for their sins and ask Christopher what they should do. He tells them to reject the false gods, Jove and Apollo, and to place their trust in the one true God, who is the source of all forgiveness. They follow his counsel and, when pretending to offer sacrifice to the gods in the temple, manage to pull down the statues of Jove and Apollo with their belts. When the king discovers their betrayal, he orders them to put to death. He has one placed in chains, hung up, and slowly dismembered. The other has her hands and legs tied and her teeth knocked out one at a time. She is then burned at the stake and, when that proves ineffective, finally beheaded. Both women die martyrs' deaths and inspire many people in the city to believe in the God of Christopher.

At this point, the king's rage focuses on Christopher himself. He orders the saint to be bound to a huge iron chair made especially for him, surrounded with wood, and set aflame in the middle of the city. To ignite the fire, the king has many vessels of oil poured over the giant's head. Although engulfed by the raging flames, Christopher survives unharmed. His victory over death enrages the king all the more. This time he decides to resort to multiple tortures to bring about the death of the dog-headed giant. He orders his soldiers to tie Christopher to a great heap of wood in front of the palace and to shoot repeated volleys of arrows at him. They do so for twelve hours straight but fail to kill him, because the wind miraculously blows all of the arrows to the left or to the right of their target, thus allowing Christopher to survive unscathed. At the end of the day, the king has Christopher taken down and put under guard lest someone try to set him free during the night.

The next morning, the king resumes the execution. As the archers begin their work, he taunts his captive and dares Christopher's God to save him from the continuous onslaught of the approaching arrows. As the words leave his lips, one of the arrows mysteriously leaps from the ground into the king's eye and blinds him. The king is in complete and utter agony. To demonstrate the power of God and his own willingness to forgive his persecutor, Christopher promises the king healing if he places over his wounded eye a paste made from a mixture of his martyred blood and some earth from his tomb. He then turns to the Lord, humbly requests that his shrine be a powerful place of intercession, and freely gives up his spirit. After Christopher's death, the king follows the saint's instructions, regains his sight in his eye, and comes to believe in the God of the Christians. The account ends with a voice from heaven affirming the power of Christopher's intercession and a reference to the many conversions for which he was responsible.

Narrative Movement

At first sight, one might be tempted to discount as simple nonsense this strange tale about a dog-headed saint, especially since it bears such little resemblance to the more popular and widespread legend of St. Christopher and the infant Jesus. When one remembers, however, that one of the primary purposes of hagiography is to build up the reader's faith, one can approach the tale from a very different perspective.[2] Rather than concentrating on the historical veracity of the story, a much more fruitful approach would be to look at the basic Gospel truths it seeks to convey.

This story renders an account of Christopher's martyrdom. It is permeated with Scriptural allusions and uses the story of Jesus as its primary point of reference. Just as Jesus, the God-man, goes to an unbelieving world to teach, heal, redeem, and sanctify, so too does Christopher, the man-beast, go to the unbelievers of the Syrian city of Samos to preach the Gospel and carry out the work of his Lord. Christopher's life is a faint but reliable reflection of Jesus'. His very name points to his mission in life. As Christopher, the "Christ-bearer," his sole purpose in life is to carry Christ to others. He does so by modeling himself entirely on Christ and by giving witness to the extraordinary power and grace of the Triune God.

The parallels between Christopher and Christ go beyond the mere similarities of their names. Both hear a voice from heaven at the time of their baptism. Both are sent to preach God's Word and to work signs and miracles in the midst of an unbelieving people. Both preach against the works of Satan and the worship of false gods. Both attract a large crowd of followers and inspire others to lay down their lives for their faith. Both give up their own lives for the sake of the Gospel and offer hope and powerful intercession after their deaths. Of course, Christopher's story is only a pale reflection of Christ's. He is not a God-man, but a man-dog. Unlike Christ, his passion and death are relatively free of suffering; nor does he rise from the dead or gloriously ascend to heaven. Christopher, moreover, is oversized and hideous-looking. He is a dog-headed giant whose very existence stands as a witness of God's ability to accomplish the impossible. If God can make a saint out of someone as outwardly grotesque as Christopher, then surely he can change the cold, monstrous hearts of an unbelieving people.

The legend's narrative movement focuses on God's power to act in the person of Christ and through his friends. Christopher's grotesque looks do not preclude him from becoming one such friend. On the contrary, they are a powerful reminder that God judges not according to outward appearances, but by the inner movements of the heart. Christopher's steadfast and faithful witness throughout the account confirms his deep attachment to Christ. As a dog is a loyal companion to its master, Christopher, the dog-headed saint, is a devoted and trustworthy friend of Christ. Christopher's reward for this steadfast loyalty is the great intercessory power granted him both during and after his earthly sojourn. He whose animal tongue produces human speech uses that tongue after his death to intercede for all who come to him in need. The power of Christopher's prayer is rooted in the power of God. The saint bears not only Christ's name, but also his power. He uses that power on Christ's behalf to bestow God's favors on all those who seek and ask with a sincere heart.

An Array of Symbols

In addition to a narrative movement patterned after the life of Christ, this version of the Christopher legend also contains a number of important symbols: the voice from heaven, a flowering staff, the hybrid saint, the evil king, the false gods, the multiple tortures, and the miraculous tomb---to name but a few. These symbols possess various levels of meaning and help to convey some of the legend's deep spiritual meaning.

1. A voice from heaven, a sign of the saint's special favor with God, is heard at both the beginning and the end of the legend. At the beginning, this voice comes in conjunction with a cloud that descends from heaven and hovers above the saint. It identifies Christopher as a specially chosen servant, who has been baptized in the name of the Holy Trinity. At the end, the voice identifies the martyred Christopher as a faithful servant and powerful intercessor for all who turn to him in need. The symbolic meaning of the voice comes through very clearly. From the moment of his baptism, Christopher has found favor with God. After his death, he is allowed to share that favor with others through the power of intercessory prayer.

2. One of Christopher's first actions after entering the Syrian city of Samos is to plant his staff in the ground and ask the Lord to make it flower. As a result, the staff bears an

abundance of verdant foliage. This action of Christopher's is rife with symbolism. It is an allusion to the planting of the cross on Golgotha ("the place of the Skull"), where Jesus died in reparation for the sins of humanity. The staff's rich leafage deepens this symbolism by connecting it also with the tree of life. Like Jesus' cross, Christopher's staff transforms the dead and barren into something new and life-giving. Because it is a staff, however, it also represents humanity's difficult journey through life and its constant need for firm support. As such, it highlights the importance of being rooted at all times in the redeeming power of the cross, itself a powerful symbol of Christ's paschal mystery. Once again, the symbolism is clear. As the patron saint of travelers, Christopher offers that support by bearing Christ to others throughout their pilgrim journey through life. He does so from baptism to the tomb---and at all points in between.

3. The legend stands out for its reference to Christopher as a "dog-headed saint," that is, as someone comprised of two distinct natures---part man and part dog. As pointed out earlier, this union of human and animal natures is a distant and very vague (even corrupted) reflection of the union of human and divine natures in the person of Christ, the standard after which Christopher actively (albeit ever so poorly) models his life. On another level, however, the image of a "dog-headed" saint brings to mind the well-known Christian metaphor of spiritual growth as a movement from the *animal* to the *rational* to the *spiritual* states.[3] Through the grace of God, Christopher has been able to integrate in his life all three of these states into a single, harmonious whole. He is a "holy dog-man," someone whose passionate, rational, and spiritual sides peaceably coexist as a result of his cooperation with the ongoing influence of God's

transforming grace. When seen from this perspective, what appears as a monstrosity to human eyes is a powerful symbol of human conversion and a visible sign of God's power to redeem and sanctify.

4. The legend also contrasts the saintly actions of the dog-headed saint with the luxurious life yet monstrous actions of the evil King Dagnus. Throughout the tale, the king seeks to convert Christopher to the worship of his gods, Jove and Apollo. His attempts fail miserably and even backfire, since Christopher still manages to convert many of the royal soldiers and subjects to the Christian faith. A spiritual battle goes on throughout the tale between Dagnus and his false gods and Christopher and the living God. Since Jove and Apollo are presented as powerless and ineffectual, the only resources the king has to offset the holy influence of Christopher are imprisonment, torture, and eventual execution. Throughout the tale, these evil actions are depicted as the work of the devil. God's grace enables Christopher, the dog-man, to withstand this evil to the end, for he has reached a level of sanctify not previously thought possible for the race of dog-headed people. Rich and powerful as he may be, Dagnus, by way of contrast, succumbs to his darker side, and acts on behalf of the evil one.

5. The true monstrosity of the tale appears not in Christopher's outward appearance, but in the multiple tortures used by the king to punish those who defy him. He beheads some 400 soldiers. He has one woman hung up and dismembered. He binds another woman, knocks her teeth out one at a time, and tries to burn her at the stake. When that fails, he has her beheaded. Christopher, too, is subjected to multiple tortures. After the king tries unsuccessfully to set him aflame, he faces a firing squad of archers for hours

on end. When the king fails to execute him, he has him closely guarded and resumes his seemingly futile efforts the very next day. These multiple tortures serve two purposes in the tale. In the first place, they demonstrate the terrible extent to which the king will go to achieve his evil ends. In the second place, they reveal God's power and show how it is at work even in the most trying of circumstances. To be sure, the courage of a martyr in the face of death is just as much a sign of divine power as a miraculous survival from fiery flames. God can bring good out of all events and circumstances, even the hideous and monstrous actions of an evil king.

6. At the end of the story, the evil King Dagnus goes to Christopher's tomb, regains sight in his eye, and converts to the Christian faith. This is but the first of many such miracles and conversion stories that takes place through the powerful intercession of the dog-headed saint. Because of Christopher, King Dagnus, who in the story represents the epitome of evil, comes to his senses, forsakes his false gods, and embraces Jesus Christ as his Lord and master. Such a conversion points to the power of God's grace to penetrate the darkness of the human heart. If Dagnus can be converted, anyone can. The God of Christopher, the dog-headed saint, is the God of impossible things. Christopher's tomb, in turn, is a powerful symbol of hope, a constant reminder to those who believe in God's willingness to intervene on their behalf. According to the legend, what Christopher accomplishes during his life pales in comparison to the miracles he will perform and the conversions he will effect afterwards. Through his powerful gift of intercession, Christopher bears Christ to others and encourages them to do the same.

Conclusion

The legend of Christopher, the dog-headed saint, attracts today's reader because of the monstrous size and grotesque appearance of its principle protagonist and the imaginative use of narrative and symbol to convey some of the most fundamental truths of the Christian faith. Although it possesses little historical worth, its value as a piece of hagiographical literature, the primary purpose of which is to deepen the reader's faith, is much more readily recognized.

When the reader interprets the various symbols in this legend spiritually, the narrative comes alive and edifies in new and meaningful ways. Christopher represents every person who bears Christ in his or her heart and allows God's grace to integrate the passionate, rational, and spiritual powers of the human soul. The voice heard both at his baptism at the beginning of the tale and at his tomb at the end is the voice of God that each person must strive to listen to in the inner sanctum of his or her heart. His pilgrim's staff is the cross each person must carry in his or her difficult journey through life, one that must be firmly planted in the ground of one's soul if the saving mystery it represents is to flower and bring forth life. The hideous and monstrous actions of King Dagnus represent the evil that will come from anyone who allows the forces of darkness to take root in the heart. Like Dagnus, all are called to come to their senses, to cast aside false gods (whatever they may be), and embrace the God of Christopher. Like Christopher and those he converted, all are called to trust in God and face the future with courage and steadfast hope. To this end, the tomb of the dog-headed saint reminds the reader not only of death, but also of what lies beyond it. It also points to the power of prayer and the need all have to identify their needs and present them to God and the communion of saints.

The God of Christopher, the dog-headed saint, is the God of the impossible. Those who believe in this God never lose hope and believe that even those who perform the most hideous and monstrous of crimes are not beyond the pale of God's transforming grace. The legend of Christopher is about God's power to cast out darkness from the human heart and to give people hope that, regardless of what they look like, where they come from, or what they have done, they too might be bearers of Christ to those around them. It edifies us by reminding us that, even though we will most likely never make it onto the Church's liturgical calendar, we are all called to sanctity and to be numbered among God's closest and most intimate of friends.

Notes

1   Iconography of Christopher, the dog-headed saint, and versions of his legend (BHL 1764; BHL 1766) can be found on the Internet at: http://www.ucc.ie/milmart/Christopher.html [Accessed on November 11, 2007]. The narrative followed in this essay is that of BHL 1766.

2   See Hippolyte Delehaye, *The Legends of the Saints: An Introduction to Hagiography*, trans. V.M. Crawford (Notre Dame, Ind., University of Notre Dame Press, 1961), 2.

3   See, for example, William of St. Thierry, *The Golden Epistle*, nos. 41-92, 195-300, Cistercian Fathers Series 12 (Kalamazoo: Mich.: Cistercian Publications, 1980), 25-42, 78-105.

Liturgical Formation as an Agent of Transformation

Robin P P Gibbons

The situation

The prophets of doom who foretold the demise of Christianity at the end of the 20th Century seem to have had their expectations dashed, or at least put on hold! It is true that various academics and other writers such as the Oxford academic Professor Richard Dawkins and the journalist, Christopher Hitchens amongst them, see religion purely as a construct of human life and not necessarily a benevolent force.[1] Nevertheless, it is also true that religion is still a huge part of human experience and life throughout the world. Even in those countries where secularism has fully taken hold of societal structures, the influence of particular religious traditions runs deep. As Rowan Williams commented in his book, *Why Study The Past?* (DLT 2005), globalisation and ease of communication means that we face articulate religious systems that cannot simply accept Western modernity's 'rational and universal triumph'.[2] His comment is particularly focussed in the ongoing situation of the Church in European culture:

> Christian history is part of modernity's buried and frequently denied biography. To disinter some of this biography is not only something that makes for the health of the Church: It is a seriously needed contribution to the intellectual

and emotional well-being of the culture...That witness has to do with a promise of universal community that is grounded not in assumptions about universal right and reason but in a narrative displaying how communication is made possible between strangers by a common relatedness to God's presence and act in history.[3]

In the debates about the constitution of the European Union at the beginning of the 21st century, the Catholic Church in particular and other groups such as Germany's Central Jewish Council, forcibly reminded the member States that the origins of our present European civilisation lies in that Christian tradition.[4] This is very much part of the thinking of Pope Benedict XVI and underpinned his concern for a new evangelisation of Europe, a theme returned to in many of his speeches. In the now famous lecture given in the *Aula Magna* of Regensberg University on September 12th, 2006, he said:

> The inner rapprochement between Biblical faith and Greek philosophical enquiry was an event of decisive importance not only from the standpoint of the history of religions, but also from that of world history-it is an event which concerns us even today. Given this convergence, it is not surprising that Christianity, despite its origins and some significant developments in the East, finally took on its historically decisive character in Europe. We can also express this the other way around: This convergence, with the subsequent addition of Roman heritage, created Europe and remains the foundation of what can rightly be called Europe.[5]

The Pope, like Archbishop Rowan Williams, challenges even the most hardened secularist to acknowledge the historical influence of Christianity and to focus on what precisely Europe (and by extension the Global community) is about in its enlarged vision of membership. It was the omission of the term "God" from the proposed Constitution that drew the most criticism from the Catholic Church. Whatever the rights and wrongs of political debate the concern expressed by the Church stems in part from a desire to establish a fundamental truth, viz., that Christianity has been formative in the evolution of Europe and its peoples. This is not to hide or brush out some of the less agreeable aspects of religious belief and practice, but it is an acknowledgement that the history of our world in both particular and general aspects needs to be fully comprehended and understood in truth!

Patterns of global migration, including immigration to and within Europe, have shown that even in a new situation, different nationals still hold religion as an important part of their daily life. This strong religious faith has sometimes caused tension within countries of immigration, especially with those who espouse a secular state. A particular example (though not an exclusive one) is the clash with Islamic fundamentalism. In Great Britain, recent migrants from Eastern Europe have led to a rapid growth in the number of Catholics in certain areas of the country. This has posed quite a challenge. Ruth Gledhill, *the (London) Times'* religious correspondent, wrote an article in February 2007 in which she indicated that the rapid growth of Roman Catholics, especially from Poland in the UK, now meant that Catholicism was set to overtake Anglicanism as the leading Church.[6] This is also true of other Catholics from the Eastern rite, as well as Oriental Christians. One important fact that needs to be reiterated is that the Church, for many migrants, becomes a major social point of contact as well as a stable connection with their homeland and religious practice. For this reflection it is important to understand that acts of worship (liturgy) and prayer play a highly significant part in this process. There is the hint here that, whatever we may think about liturgy, it has in an evidential way been part of a method of creating community.

It is evident from the vast interest in anything to do with religion, especially the rather sensational aspects, that there is a still a hunger for knowledge and information amongst people about faith, God, and religious belief. Alongside this thirst for knowledge and meaning is an acknowledgement that the Churches need to be more proactive in teaching and communicating their message. If we take the example of one history, we have in British culture a huge Christian legacy, not only implicit in our laws and systems but in the art and architecture we inherit. The problem is that since the apparent collapse of organised religion there are fewer people who have the ability to interpret the vocabulary of belief and its symbol structures. In a society with a significant generational gap between people who have had firsthand experience of religion, and large numbers of people who have had little or no contact with any organised religion at all, the lack of people having any ability to comprehend these systems means a significant difficulty for the Church in trying to evangelise and teach the message of the Gospel. This general lack of knowledge, what we can term the lack of religious vocabulary, needs to be tackled if our Churches are to speak and work effectively in the challenging circumstances of the present day. That there is a need for good communication cannot be doubted, but it also requires communities to organise and inform themselves in an articulate, knowledgeable and theological manner. One of the great disservices that one can do for others is to let 'misinformation' happen without challenge. At certain times it would seem that those who are the detractors of religion have had more than their fair share of influence, not helped by an inadequate response from the Churches. One of our great contemporary British theologians, Keith Ward, in his book, *Is Religion Dangerous* (Lion 2006) points out:

> We cannot eliminate religions, they are here to stay. It is possible to make them powerful forces for creative living, moral motivation and human reconciliation. It may be that only reliance on a spiritual power can motivate unlimited love, forgiveness and compassion, or offer hope to a world

so lost in hatred and greed.[7]

Where do we begin? My own instinct is to start examining what it means to be a Christian and to look at where we most connect with God, Church, and faith. For those who practise this faith the simple answer to that would be in our liturgy, that is to say, those acts of worship that constitute the regular coming together in faith of a people with their God.

The Importance of Liturgy

The popular picture of empty churches with an elderly congregation worshipping Sunday by Sunday in an archaic and outmoded form of ritual is a total distortion of the facts. It is true that there are small and struggling congregations, but then there are also large and vibrant communities full of young (and old) people. The varieties of religious worship on any given Sunday in the British Isles would be astonishing if it were not true, i.e., Evangelical, Orthodox, traditional Catholic and Anglican, Pentecostal, Charismatic, Cathedral, House Church, the list is endless. It is in these gatherings that the life of the Church is to be experienced, but it is also our task to make these gatherings not only better known by others but understood in a fuller and better way, especially in a theological and ecclesial manner, by those who are involved in worship.

Not every act of liturgy is good! There are times in the life of any church when the celebration fails to resonate with the people or, because of different expectations, the act of worship fails to connect. It might also be bad planning or music, a bad sermon, or bad aesthetics that fails to lift the spirit. The list is not endless, but there are things that make for bad liturgy, as the late Mark Searle so ably summed up:

> Religious privatism and massification (sic), radical individualism and civil religion are the divisive forces with which the liturgy and catechesis must contend if a genuine

community of worship is to be built up...We go with theses forces because we know no other way, so that even the communitarian language and practices of our tradition are reinterpreted, quite unconsciously, to conform to our cultural expectations[8].

On the other hand, when an act of worship connects with the celebrants (in the widest sense of the whole assembly at prayer) ,when the music lifts the heart, and the Word of God, heard and preached, touches the spirit, then something transformative takes place; we become part of God's people gathered in God's name and present to the Triune God. Part of our task is to discover and understand the components that enable this transformation to take place. The root of the word liturgy comes from the Greek, *leitos* and *ergon*, literally the people's work. Whatever the discussion on the etymology of the word itself, it suggests that somehow in the Christian context, liturgy is never something done for us by a group of specialists or one knowledgeable individual. Rather, it is a common work and duty, that is an identification of liturgy as the work of God and ourselves in Christ, done by us together, for the life of the world. The ancient axiom, attributed to Prosper of Aquitaine(390-455), *lex supplicandi legem statuat credendi*, often quoted in a shortened form as, *lex orandi est lex credendi*, places the liturgical act (the rule of prayer) as the first connection with the doctrine and theology of the Church (the rule of faith); in other words the act of worship is not secondary to theology or doctrine but part of it and deeply connected to it.

Aidan Kavanagh in his seminal work, *On Liturgical Theology* (1992) [9] has this to say: "The liturgy of the faithful Christians is the primary theological act of the Church itself."[10] What Kavanagh means, is that the liturgy is itself a primary theology, having itself various component parts: "festive, ordered, steeped in the arts, canonical, and eschatological."[11] This requires anybody involved or interested in liturgy to investigate these components in order to understand precisely what the liturgical act is about. Part of Kavanagh's research and insight has been to promote a particular appreciation of Liturgical Theology and to rescue it from simply being an adjunct of Doctrine, Sacramental, or Pastoral Theology, He is not alone; there are (and have been) a growing number of scholars who in recent years have helped develop the study and understanding of liturgy worship in many different contexts. Nevertheless, this academic work needs to be translated from academic study into the pastoral formation of people in liturgy and ‚perhaps better still, 'for' liturgy. Returning to one of Kavanagh's themes, one that he maintains with great vigour, that people cannot just go out and 'do' liturgy with little preparation. It has to be experienced, celebrated, and understood over a period of time. This is one of the current dilemmas of our various churches. The sense of urgency often generated about our perceived and apparent need to grow and appear relevant to society often means that a quick solution is advocated. Too often when the question of relevancy rears its head, especially in the context of numbers and age, and in the drive to accommodate and reach out to a hungry world, new liturgical formats and experiences are tried, often without adequate knowledge and understanding. Kavanagh describes the liturgy as a social occasion, which of its very nature is repetitious and rhythmical; that is why the liturgical texts in the older churches are often invariable, having what he calls a unifying function (to gather and form the community into the people of God). Writing about the context of Anglican debates on presidency of the Eucharist, Rowan Williams underscores this need to work in a more ecclesiological and liturgical mode and to discover what he terms a 'grammar' of recognisability:

> The requirement that the eucharist is celebrated by an ordained minister is not about the powers of the ministry but about the catholicity of the congregation, its proper openness and recognisability to the wider church, so that

the eucharist is more than the prayer of the group alone... Without some means of identifying this local action with the act of the whole Church and of Christ in his whole Body, we weaken (fatally?) the model of the Church as a network of mutual dependence and mutual acknowledgement.[12]

In order to further ground the experience of liturgy and prevent it from becoming a spectacle or performance, we note that the liturgy is governed by a number of canons (rules), part of the grammar of recognisability, amongst which Kavanagh lists four in particular: Firstly that of Scripture, 'what the community deems it appropriate that it should read and hear as it stands before God in worship'[13]. Secondly the canon of baptismal faith summed up in the Trinitarian creeds, which 'constrains the assembly to worship in such a way that its apostolate in the world as an icon of the Holy Trinity and agent under God of the world's communion with its source is rendered accessible to those of good will'.[14] In particular this will help prevent too much individualism to grow, because it throws us back on our common baptismal vocation to be a chosen race, a royal priesthood, a holy nation, God's people who exist to declare the wonderful deeds of God who has called us from darkness into his marvelous light. (1 Peter 2:9) Thirdly, there is the canon of Eucharistic faith, perhaps more familiar to those communities who have as their central celebration the Holy Communion, Mass, Eucharist or Divine Liturgy, but which has a great lesson to give all our churches.

In the texts and prayers of the Eucharist, especially the 'repertoire' of anaphora's or Eucharistic Prayers (canons), there is a distillation of the revealed Gospel and its theology concerning the truth and presence of Christ, 'within the corporate person of him whose Gospel is in motion for the life of the world'.[15] Lastly .there is the body of canonical law itself, not so much the regulating policeman of ceremony and ritual, but rather the guarantor of authenticity and good practice. The tendency in history has been to oscillate between over-regulation (rubric) and rejection of law, but we cannot ignore this necessary part of Church order, for if we do, the context of liturgical action begins to drift away from the churches life and gets honoured more in the breach than in observance. If one can appreciate that the rules guiding worship are there to help fix all the elements into Christian life, then we can begin to appreciate that, rather than be a burden, laws, if correctly understood and interpreted, are often of great help in the practice of worship.

Kavanagh places the understanding and formation of people in all aspects of liturgy as an essential feature of mission. This comes from his understanding of the primary function of liturgy in the life of the church, namely that, 'The liturgy of the faithful Christians is the primary theological act of the Church itself'.[16] This engages us in a task of both holding on to the heritage stemming from our Judeo-Christian tradition in order to draw on its wealth and experience, and at the same time engaging in the world and learning from it as well. Another great liturgical theologian, Romano Guardini (1885-1968), put it succinctly when he wrote: 'One must create a Theology which flows out of the basic realities of scripture, the fundamental content of Church, and the essence of human life, within a language that contemporary theologians and believers hold in common'.[17] However Guardini, as with Kavanagh, also recognised the challenges facing the Christian community with the development of human culture and technological change. He wondered if the Christian liturgy was too wedded to ancient structures to be able to adapt, and in particular if the individualism and self-sufficiency of modern society might prevent accessibility to a communitarian liturgy. Our potential to engage in liturgy depends on many things; 'The lack of fruitful and lofty culture causes spiritual life to grow numb and narrow; the lack of the subsoil of healthy nature makes it develop on mawkish, perverted, and unlawful lines'.[18]

In this sense, the four guiding canons of Kavanagh do provide one useful hermeneutic by which we can start to examine how our liturgical life measures up. One can recognise in Guardini's 'mawkish, perverted, and unlawful lines', not only any number of liturgical experiments of the past few decades but also the relentless neo-conservatism of particular focus groups. Nevertheless, there is a definite challenge, one Anglican Bishop was heard to opine at a 'confirmation', that twenty-first-century people just did not care for sacramental worship, and therefore it is incumbent upon us to find other ways of expressing our faith. His comment was more a reflection on the social and demographic changes affecting the dispersed rural communities in the West of England than a true assessment of the spiritual life of the community itself, but it is the type of comment heard from many clergy who, facing the onslaught of change do not know what to do. But we do not have to reinvent the wheel; we need instead to form people in what already exists, so that we can then adapt and inculturate where necessary, knowing that in doing so we are not throwing out the baby with the bath water.

Liturgy and Society

One of the tasks of the Christian Church is mission; in terms of liturgical life this is to re-engage with the rich treasure we have and to seek ways of reinvigorating the structures of worship already present in the vast reservoir of tradition. Contemporary life seeks for meaning at all kinds of levels and, even in the activities of daily life, the echoes of what we as Christians do still resonate. It is not difficult to notice how in the new 'cathedrals' of prosperity, the great shopping malls, a seasonal quality is used in décor, music and ambience, to encourage us to shop and tarry more. The liturgical cycle is paralleled in these places; there is a 'baptismal area', those spaces set around a great pool or splashing fountain, or communion areas, the coffee shops and café places. If liturgy is a social and ritual act then human beings are essentially 'liturgical' without often fully realising it. We still act out the pattern of birthday parties, we spend a lot of time and money on all aspects of weddings and, in the secular society, an absence of a coherent theology of death has resulted in the phenomenon of mourning and passing rituals becoming ever more complex as if trying to atone for the lack of comprehension. These are not enemies of faith but partners to be drawn in through the medium of liturgical worship. Many people are fascinated by the rituals and acts of the Church because the simple fact is that they have not often come across these celebrations; they are to all intents and purposes outside the vocabulary of ordinary experiences. It is interesting to note how, in an age of supposed indifference to the traditional Christian teaching about marriage, the 'church' wedding is still very popular, and those involved spend vast amounts of money on the occasion; the décor, dress and 'liturgical' structure of the event are meticulously prepared.

This does not mean that the symbolism and theology of the rite are any better understood, but there in these occasions there is a residual attempt to connect with something beyond themselves. Weddings and funerals are often the only times many people will come into contact with the Church. In the case of funerals the expectations are different; bereavement and grief give to those dealing with the liturgy an important task, for it is often the minister, priest, or vicar's task to guide and lead the family and friends through services that are unfamiliar but which nevertheless provide an important sense of identity and meaning. It is all the more important that those involved in any of these pastoral offices be trained carefully in all the aspects of worship, so that we are sensitive to the pastoral care of the bereaved, but nevertheless proclaim the Christian message at the heart of the rite itself. One has only to look at the roadside 'shrines' marking a fatal accident spot, that have recently become a feature of British life, to realise that ritual and symbol are not lost to people: they use aromatic oil to anoint their bodies, incense to burn and smell, have ritualised gatherings to celebrate an anniversary, and wear festive clothes to mark a celebration. Rather, it is often those of us involved in the official business of 'church' that have not been brave or far-sighted enough to reach out and use what we already possess in a fuller manner. Do we splash about in the baptismal pool? Does our bread resemble real bread, or our oil anoint us fully? Do we really use light and sound to best advantage, to really use movement and gesture? Do we try to connect with the 'spirituality' of the people in order to integrate and link it to the liturgy? Romano Guardini in his classical work on liturgical theology, *Vom Geist der Liturgie*[19] (1918*)*, advocated liturgical reform but warned against faith being subsumed into the culture of the day. He then encouraged those involved in the Christian life to discover the grace of God at work (mediated) through the contemporary world in all its forms. He is cautious about any artificial division between liturgy and life: 'There could be no greater mistake than that of discarding the valuable elements in the spiritual life of the people for the sake of liturgy, or than the desire of assimilating them to it'[20]; words that still need to be taken to heart by many engaged in liturgical renewal.

Perhaps it is because the legacy of the past still rambles on through our sectarian divisions that we shy away from symbols, but to continue to do so will result in an inward-looking and insular group of Christian communities. The divisions of the past have to be reconciled, and it will have to be done through the medium of the liturgy in all its aspects for it to have any meaning at all.

Formation for Church and Community

Liturgical formation in its widest sense will have to deal with our relationship to world and society, but apart from that outreach, formation will always be a necessary component of growth in Christian life. Nearly all our major church denominations have liturgical groups of some kind or another, we all have service books or at least guide lines for worship, and in recent years a remarkable convergence has taken place between various liturgical groups. In particular the work of the Liturgical Movement, which bore fruit in the Second Vatican Council of the Roman Catholic Church, has shaped attitudes to liturgy ever since. But in recent years, the heady optimism of the sixties and seventies has been challenged by a variety of forces, some of which look back to another era and urge restoration of what had once been, whilst others have gone their own separate way, either moving outside the institution or ignoring it. The task is to place liturgy where it belongs: at the heart of our lives as Christians. It is also to understand it utilising all the different components that it brings together; implicit in this is a great theological enterprise. One of the great Orthodox liturgists of the twentieth century, Father Alexander Schmemann, in his work, *Introduction to Liturgical Theology* (1986), placed before people what he saw as the task and method of such a theology: 'If liturgical theology stems from an understanding of worship as the public act of the Church, then its final goal will be to clarify and explain the connection between this act and the Church, i.e., to explain how the Church expresses and fulfils herself in this act'.[21] This is very much akin to Guardini's perception that renewal could only take place when we discover the essence of the liturgy and its centrality on the Triune God through Christ and the Spirit, and fully and freely engage with the world. Schmemann's exploration of Liturgical Theology reminds us that the liturgy has always been developmental, but that development is never whimsical or arbitrary, it depends on a fidelity to what both Schmemann and Kavanagh understand as the 'rule of prayer' or Rowan Williams as the 'grammar' of responsibility. Kavanagh as we have noted, amplifies this into four constituent 'canons'; Schmemann begins with an insistence that history must be a starting point but: not become an end in itself, but rather the beginning of further exploration. After that initial reflection must come theological synthesis, that is the interpretation of the rule of prayer:

> In our liturgical practice there are things which to many

people seem to be the age-old tradition of the Church, but which in fact distort this tradition. It is impossible to discern them outside their historical perspective, without comparing facts…But after historical analysis must come a theological synthesis…the elucidation of the rule of prayer as the rule of faith.[22]

Formation in liturgy is a complex task, because it involves a number of critical components, but complexity does not mean that it has to be difficult, rather that we should engage in the task with great carefulness. Too often it has been seen as the preserve of those training for ministry, though one might be forgiven for wondering what exactly some of those in ministerial activity learnt about liturgy, but it is not. If we return to that primary theology which understands liturgy as the work of the whole people of God, then formation in liturgy is the duty of each one of us. This is not a new thing; St Cyril of Jerusalem, in his lectures on the Christian Sacraments, told his fourth-century audience that learning was part of Christian life: For Cyril, the experience of the mysteries, the liturgies of Baptism, Chrismation and Eucharist was to be explained to the candidates before their initiation, but also followed by further catechesis as they experienced the liturgy:

> On former times of our meeting together ye have heard sufficiently, by the loving kindness of God, concerning Baptism, and Chrism, and the partaking of the Body and Blood of Christ; and now it is necessary to pass on to the next in order, meaning today to give finish to your spiritual edification. [23]

This is the task of formation, to examine and help others learn about the value and significance of the liturgy, not as a branch of anything else but as a subject in its own right; essentially, it is reexamination of our roots, to understand what it is we do when we are busy at the 'work of the people of God'.

Notes

1. See Dawkins, R.2007. 2nd editon. *The God Delusion.* Black Swan. Hitchens, C.2007. *God Is Not Great: The Case Against Religion.* Atlantic Books, but also the apologists such as McGrath, A.2007. *The Dawkins Delusion?; Atheist Fundamentalism and the Denial of the Divine.* London. SPCK and Ward, Keith.2006. *Is Religion Dangerous?* Oxford. Lion Hudson.

2. Williams, Rowan. 2005. *Why Study History?* London. Darton, Longman and Todd. p. 113

3. Williams. 2005. p. 113

4. 'God missing from EU Constitution', BBC News, World Edition , 2003 http://news.bbc.co.uk

5. Benedict XVI lecture; *Faith, Reason and The University: Memories and Reflections.* Aula Magna. Regensburg University, Germany, September 12 2006

6. Ruth Gledhill, Article in the Times Feb 15th 2007. *Catholics set to pass Anglicans as leading UK Church.*

7. Ward, K. 2006. p.199

8. Searle, Mark. *Private Religion, Individualistic Society, Common Worship.* In Eleanor Bernstein, C.S.J., Ed. 1990. *Liturgy and Spirituality in Context: Perspectives on Prayer and Culture.* The Liturgical Press, Collegeville. p.35

9. Kavanagh, Aidan.1992. *On Liturgical Theology.* The Liturgical Press, Collegeville.

10. Kavanagh, A. *On Liturgical Theology*, Section 4 p. 97 in Vogel, D Ed.2000. *Primary Sources of Liturgical Theology.* Pueblo. USA

11. Vogel p. 96

12. Williams, R. 2006. p. 107

13. Vogel p. 94

14. Kavanagh text in Vogel p. 94

15. Vogel p. 96

16 Vogel p. 95

17 Krieg , R.A. 2001. *Romano Guardini: A Precursor of Vatican II*. Notre Dame Press Indiana. P 203

18 Krieg p. 89

19 Guardini, R. 1918. *Vom Geist der Liturgie*.Frieburg. Herder. English translation Guardini, R and Pierce,J.M.1998. *The Spirit of The Liturgy (Milestones of Catholic Theology)*. Crossroad Publishing Co.

20 Quoted in Krieg, R.A.2001. p. 81

21 Schmemann, A. 1986.*Introduction to Liturgical Theology*. Crestwood. N.Y. St Vladimir's Seminary Press . p. 17.

22 Schmemann p. 20

23 St. Cyril of Jerusalem. *Lectures on The Christian Sacraments*. Edited by F.L. Cross.1980. SPCK. London . Mystagogical Catechesis V. p. 71

Dying as "The Journey Home"
Ann V. Graber

To everything there is a season,
and a time to every purpose under heaven:
A time to be born, and a time to die.[1]

In our increasingly urban culture, the natural rhythm of life and death is no longer observable as it was in our agrarian past. As we removed ourselves more and more from living in rhythm with the cycles of nature, we also distanced ourselves from the miracle of birth and the witnessing of death.

A friend from Norway told me that, according to Norwegian folklore, dying used to be a communally accepted part of life. She described the custom surrounding the event as follows:

> When Ola became too old or sick to leave his bed, family, friends, and neighbors would gather outside, open his windows and begin calling to his soul, "Come on, Ola, leave your old sick body! Let your soul fly free! Come on out, Ola, join your friends!" And ..., sooner or later, Ola would leave his body and expire. When the body could no longer sustain life, it was time to die. That's the way it was done in olden times.[2]

By contrast, in our contemporary technological society, death is an uncomfortable subject. By and large, we treat it as something that must be deferred at all cost, or denied. In times of crisis involving death or dying, family and friends may be ill equipped to help due to their own uncertainty and attendant shock. When the inevitable comes to pass, often professionals — in various secular and religious capacities — are called upon for assistance.

At this writing, it is statistically determined that in the US 60% of people die in hospitals, 20% in nursing homes, and only about 20% die at home.[3] We can readily see that we have not only separated ourselves from death and dying, but by relegating the care of the dying to professionals, we have lost the intimacy that attended the dying process. At a time when a person may need the ministrations of family and friends the most, he or she is largely separated from them and isolated in an unfamiliar place. The hospital setting is, by and large, impersonal. Consequently, when a terminally ill person checks into a hospital, he or she becomes a "patient" — individuality, even personhood is compromised. There may be help available for alleviating some of the physical symptoms, but is there care of the soul, of one's uniqueness and individuality?

In part, adjustments in how we approach death were brought about by industrialization and the consequent mobility of our society. However, the biggest cause for our changed attitude toward death is due to the fact that in earlier times people died faster of either acute illnesses or physical injuries. There were few cures for diseases or injury repairs available. Improved medical technology vastly changed how, when, and where we died. Now only about 10% of the US population die sudden deaths; the remaining 90% die over extended periods of time. Many acute illnesses are now curable while others are treatable as chronic diseases. This has prolonged the process of dying, but has not changed the inevitability of death.

The phenomenal growth of the Hospice Movement in recent years provides ample evidence that we are in dire need of help when it comes to end-of-life issues. The holistic approach Hospice employs of addressing the needs of a dying person, inclusive of physical, psychosocial, and spiritual needs, speaks well for valuing wholeness. Respecting the humanity of the dying person and encouraging closeness to family and loved ones, removes some of the anxiety experienced.[4] Those who can accept the probability of impending death, in spite of the anguish it may cause, are preparing for a harmonious departure for their *journey home*.

"Home!" The very sound of the word evokes in us eternal yearnings for a safe haven: a place of refuge and protection from harm, a place of warmth, comfort, and familiarity. It speaks of love and enduring relationships. For some, it may evoke nostalgia for a place they once knew: for others, a projection toward a heavenly home. For those who come to view dying as *the journey home*, the powerful attributes of "home" beckon invitingly. The journey, although it may be painful, is experienced as a return to a longed-for state. Intuitive knowing whispers: "After a long and eventful absence, I am returning to my source of origin — experiences richer, hopefully wiser. I will no longer be a stranger in a strange world, but a citizen in my own country of spirit. There I can enjoy the companionship of others of like mind and soul. All is well, I am going home!"

Preparing Oneself to Assist Others

The noted Viennese psychiatrist and philosopher, Dr. Viktor Frankl, was asked during a TV interview, "How do you prepare someone to die?"

"I wouldn't venture to prepare anyone else to die, unless I had first prepared myself. My patients know exactly when what I say is authentic and when it is not," replied Dr. Frankl.[5]

From the above statement we can see that we will have to come to terms with our own mortality first in order to be comfortable in the presence of death or the dying. This may come from direct experience, from one's faith, or from conscious preparation for the task. Ideally, we would want to live each day as if it could be our last. Then there would be less *angst* to confront as our mortal life comes to an end.

The theme, *The Journey Home,* invariably deals with the great equalizer, death. There is no greater single event humanity has in common. Even birth, it can be argued, has its disparity. Conversely, when approaching death, we are all headed for the great unknown. We have our own fears to face and, in spite of them, preparations to make, especially when preparing to assist others.

Dr. Elisabeth Lukas, a foremost Franklian psychotherapist, challenged her colleagues to dare to stand by in empathy when a cure for the patient is no longer possible by stating:

> Faith in God has been shaken in many people's lives, and interpersonal support even more so. In our loneliness we seek from strangers what we can no longer find in a firm faith or from people close to us. Psychotherapists, this 'last hope,' cannot afford to say 'Here I cannot help, this goes beyond my field of competence.' Where the scientific knowledge fails, humanity must take over. At the limits of understanding, empathy must find words. [6]

She concluded by saying that therapists who limit themselves to what is curable, practice their profession but fail in their vocation.

As sobering as the aforementioned statements may be, they also imply that no other work is better suited to help us face our own human frailties and our own mortality. Nothing lends itself more to tending our own inner growth than being present to others on their journey through suffering. Assisting others to prepare for their transition, to help them find acceptance and peace, has its own rewards.

To that end, it is well to be acquainted with the teachings of those whom we hold in high esteem as luminaries among humankind, past and present. They include the revelators of the world's religions, as well as philosophers, poets, mystics, and many others. Some of our heroes may live in stories or fables. We may have examples in our own family history of peaceful transitions following a life courageously lived with its hardships bravely borne. The lives of "saints" and ordinary decent people abound in accounts of nobility of spirit and fearless deaths. Many of them have insights to offer that will be helpful in accepting the transitoriness of our mortal existence.

It is well documented that during a major trauma or life crisis, particularly if it involves death, people turn to their religious leaders for spiritual support and psychological help first.[7] Assistance of a religious nature necessarily implies a religious faith and, perhaps, a method of counseling. Traditionally pastors, priests, ministers, rabbis, imams, other clergy and religious have fulfilled this role within their own congregations and among the adherents of their faith. It is within their professional and vocational domain to counsel and guide them.

What is faith? No doubt, each person of faith has his or her own definition of faith. Here is one definition by a mystical poet that depicts faith eloquently:

Faith
Faith is an oasis
The caravan of reason will never reach.
(Kahlil Gibran)

Pastoral Counseling: Religion meets Psychotherapy

The faithful, who in former times would have looked to their clergy for help when confronted with death and dying, may now land at the doorstep of someone outside of their own religious persuasion.

In more recent times, counseling those in distress has expanded far beyond the province of the clergy. In addition to ministry professionals, lay people are being trained to provide both pastoral and other types of counseling. Their outreach is extending far beyond strictly denominational boundaries. The diverse field of counseling seeks to address psychological needs of persons needing help, particularly those undergoing traumatic or lasting change. Pastoral counseling, for example, is designed to fill the gap between psychiatric interventions and exclusively religious ministrations. Pastoral counseling is emerging as a vigorous new branch on the tree of human services. It endeavors to assist people in psycho-spiritual crises.

In our "melting-pot" culture of diverse ethnicity and religious plurality the pastoral counselor, especially if working in hospitals or other public institutions, will have to understand the urgent needs of those seeking help, particularly when facing death. A counseling theory will be required that is ecumenically tolerant and inclusive, not solely steeped in one's own faith orientation and exclusive of all others.

Although this discussion is primarily based on Judeo-Christian religious understanding, it includes the wider company of truth-seekers, whether they profess to belong to a church or not. The mystic, Emanuel Swedenborg, reminds us that all members of the human race belong to the *Church Universal* by virtue of their humanity. However, individual members of humanity may also elect to belong to a *Church Specific;* ideally, a church or religion that suits their development and furthers their spiritual growth.[8]

※

In my search for helpful counseling theories that addressed "life and death issues" in a significant way, the work of Viktor Frankl stood out. He is the author of the classic, *Man's Search for Meaning,* and many other books that further develop his psychotherapy. Dr. Frankl is comfortable with the thought of our transitoriness. He sees it as part of our human condition that cannot be changed, or avoided — it must be accepted. This acceptance is not passive, but becomes the motivation, the incentive, to make the most of life while we have the opportunity to do so.

Viktor Frankl portrays life as an opportunity to create one's own lasting monument through deeds accomplished, loving relationships encountered, and suffering bravely borne. In order to accomplish this within the limited time frame available in any given lifespan, we must seize the meaning of each moment and live in the present while looking to the future with hope.

In view of the relative scarcity of psychological theories that come even close to the ideals and visions most major religions hold for humanity, Dr. Frankl's counseling theory is refreshingly open to religion, optimistic, yet pragmatic. Franklian psychology includes the spiritual dimension and honors religious values. It sees the human being reaching for something beyond self, toward "ultimate meaning," or God. Frankl gives us an explanation of what he is alluding to by stating, "God is the partner of your most intimate soliloquies. Whenever you are talking to yourself in utmost sincerity and ultimate solitude—he to whom you are addressing yourself may justifiably be called God."[9] Frankl notes that a religious person would assert that these are real dialogues between himself and God, while an atheist would be equally correct in insisting that they are only monologues within his own mind. Neither would dispute the presence of *Geist* (the nucleus of personality) in such a dialogue.

Although Dr. Frankl tries very hard to stay on the scientific side of the fence that divides psychiatry and religion, he is obviously a man of deep faith, which is reflected in his counseling theory and its application. Franklian psychology looks for what is meaningful in a person's life, what is of value to an individual. Based on that, meaning-centered interventions can be offered when troubling life situations arise. Particularly when a cure is no longer likely, then comforting the suffering becomes the mandate.

This is a lofty, yet common-sense approach to life. It sees value even in suffering. When suffering is unavoidable, and we endure it courageously, it can become the crucible for heightening our sensitivity, refining our humanness, and escalating our spiritual growth. We can emerge from our trials transformed into stronger and more compassionate human beings.

Spirituality: The Common Ground

In view of the above, we can detect that there is common ground upon which religion and Franklian psychology are both planted: Their common ground is *spirituality*. Religions may value spirituality for different reasons than Frankl's psychotherapy does, yet both recognize that spirituality is the bedrock upon which their systems are founded — whether a belief system of a given religion aiming for salvation of the soul or a therapeutic system designed to heal the human psyche.

What is spirituality? *World Spirituality: An Encyclopedic History of the Religious Quest,* points out that spirituality should be distinguished from theology and the study of religion. The inner dimension of the person is called "the spirit" by certain traditions. This spiritual core is the deepest center of the person. It is here that the person is open to a transcendent dimension. It is here that the person experiences ultimate reality. [10]

Throughout history, we have wondered about our origin and our destiny. We have a deep innate yearning to belong, to feel connected to that mysterious source, and to understand our reason for being. In answer to these yearnings, beliefs concerning our existence, ideations about God, the universe and our place in it, have emerged. Over time rituals were developed — intended to bring believers closer to this mysterious source and to establish communion or oneness with it. We call these belief systems with their attendant rituals, *religions*. Religions assist their adherents to reach toward God according to their particular understanding of God. It follows then, that spirituality is innate and that religion is acquired. People may change their religion, but they retain their inherent spiritual core. Consequently, we can view the interconnectedness of these concepts as follows:

- *theology* to be the study about God, our Source;
- *religion* as a path to God, the Source of Being;
- *spirituality* as that essential human endowment that makes

the experience of God possible.

There are many ways to experience spirituality: Some are religious, some are non-religious; some are theistic in their orientation, some are non-theistic in their understanding of the Source of Being. The transformative process will take on a hopeful note if this presupposition that *spirituality is central*, and that a person's particular *religion is supplemental*, is remembered.

As professionals in some cognate field of pastoral psychology we need to be attitudinally ready and spiritually prepared before we attempt to help others face their fears of dying. We need to be at peace with the inevitability of death – our own and the deaths of others. Transforming our attitude toward death — from fear to acceptance, even anticipation of greater things to come, has been addressed by theologians, insightful philosophers, self-transcending psychotherapists, and inspired poets.

Life, The Unbelievable
Impossible, you say, that man survives
The grave— that there are other lives?

More strange, O friend, that we should ever rise
Out of the dark to walk below these skies.
Once having risen into life and light,
We need not wonder at our deathless flight.

Life is the unbelievable; but now
That this incredible has taught us how,
We can believe the all-imagining Power
That breathed the cosmos forth as a golden flower,

Had potence in his breath
To plan us new surprises beyond death—
New spaces and new goals
For the adventures of ascending souls.
(Edwin Markham)

Based on these sentiments, dying as *the journey home* is "for the adventures of ascending souls."

Accompanying Others on Their Journey

> *Where two or three*
> *are gathered together in my name,*
> *there am I in the midst of them.*[11]

This *presence*, if not explicitly, is implicitly invited by the intention to honor the spirit of God in each other. "Only union *through* love and *in* love (using the word 'love' in its widest and most real sense of 'mutual internal affinity'),... brings individuals together, not superficially and tangentially but center to center," writes Teilhard de Chardin.[12] The perceptible flow of grace that occurs when such center-to-center union can be established is truly transformative. The transcendental quality of such an encounter may well be attributed to the presence of the universal God being "in the midst of them."

Beyond being well-intentioned, even steeped in one's own faith, it is well for anyone wishing to be of service to others to have some rudimentary understanding of the needs a dying person may have. This discussion will focus on the psycho-spiritual needs, beyond the obvious physical needs. It will speak particularly to the stage in life where a "cure" is no longer likely, but comfort measures can be provided: when all that could be done to restore health has been exhausted, and the approaching death has to be faced. Ideally, let us not wait until such a time but prepare for the inevitable transition with forethought while we are able to reflect on it, and anticipate the needs that may arise. Not only the outer necessities, but also the inner, less discernible longings, need to be addressed.

The field of pastoral counseling is an intuitive art, as well as a learned craft. The counselor walks a fine line. If the craft is overdeveloped to the exclusion of the art, there is danger of it becoming rote by only going with standardized formulations. Conversely, if the art of the counseling process is overemphasized, it may become vague and directionless. Therefore, heart and head must walk hand-in-hand for genuine progress to be made in counseling.

Perceiving or assessing another's readiness to explore the subject of death with its attendant fears and anxieties is a delicate matter. Assumptions and preconceptions based on church attendance, for example, are out of place here. When one goes to do battle on these intense fronts of life, it is well to wear the armor of vulnerability and to look for the possibility of an open window in the other. To care enough to be with someone center-to-center, or soul-to-soul, requires uncommon courage and sensitivity.

It is well to approach each person as God's unique creation and expression, especially when interacting with those who are preparing to take leave from life as we know it. According to Thomas Moore, "Care of the soul… involves cultivating depth and sacredness."[13] I would like to add, in both, the pastoral counselor and counselee, psychotherapist and client, family member or friend and loved one.

Above all, the most desirable skill to cultivate, before attempting to serve others, is the *art of listening*. This is true for the professional as well as for any helper. Some have called it *being present,* others refer to it as *with-ness*. Whatever name we give it matters little. Such active listening embraces a form of spiritual intelligence, which perceives beyond ordinary cognition. It simply knows! It knows how to establish a safe space for dialogue — when dialogue is necessary. It fosters an atmosphere of tranquility and harmony that creates sacred space — where communion beyond words is possible. Listening – *the gift of attention* - more than anything, is what we need to practice when assisting others on their *journey home*.

Medical science has, in broad strokes, mapped out the accompanying psychological stages attendant to the physical decline during the dying process. The pioneering work of Dr. Elisabeth Kübler-Ross on death and dying brought to light much helpful information about the attitudes that accompany varying stages preceding the transition. Except in sudden death, these transitional stages of shifting attitudes are generally recognizable when patients are faced with a terminal diagnosis. Beginning with shock or denial, the patient generally moves through anger, bargaining with God or looking for elusive cures and experimental treatments, followed by depression before acceptance of his or her fate is reached. The intensity and duration of a prevailing attitude may differ, but there is a definite progression observable in coming to terms with one's mortality. It behooves us to be knowledgeable about these psychological adjustments leading from fear of dying to acceptance of it. This is particularly important when attending those who are in the process of dying or when comforting their loved ones.[14]

If fear of death is the greatest impediment to harmonious progress on *the journey home,* peace is its greatest facilitator. When a person has had enough time and has progressed through the previously encountered stages, there will come a time when there is neither anger nor depression about one's fate. The individual, who has been able to express and deal with feelings as they arose, who has been able to put worldly affairs in order and complete meaningful tasks, such as saying "goodbye" to loved ones, will reach a stage of acceptance and inner peace. This person will begin to contemplate the coming transition with a degree of quiet expectancy.

The *acceptance stage* should not be mistaken for an overtly happy time. It is almost devoid of feeling. It is as if pain has gone, the struggle is over, and there comes a time for the final rest before the long journey. With acceptance there comes a turning inward, often characterized by increased need for sleep. Interest in outer things diminishes. Verbal communication becomes minimal. Silence is welcome. A gentle holding of hands, a look, a touch are the most meaningful communications at this time. The transition is near.

Resignation: How sad to think that not all reach an attitude of acceptance and die peacefully. Too often, instead of going through the dynamic process of putting the finishing touches on the monument of one's life, which leads to inner peace, some take the passive route of *resignation*. Resignation is a stagnant state, devoid of the initiative to take care of the unfinished business in one's life: Life events are not being reviewed, repressed anger is not being dealt with, fears are not acknowledged, unshed tears are not being shed, completion does not occur – neither with the people in one's life, nor with the responsibilities life brought with it. Resignation tends to leave frustration, discontent, even bitterness in its wake.

Resignation may also set in when there is seemingly no one – not even a Higher Power one believes in – with whom to share these valleys of life and draw strength from the loving encounter. The suffering person can still feel totally alone and forsaken while surrounded by people who cannot or will not "gather together" in the spirit of caring understanding.

Transformation

If we choose to do all that we can do when faced with an unchangeable fate or loss, we will eventually surrender into *acceptance* and find peace in spite of our fate – knowing that we have done our best. If, however, we just *resign* ourselves without participating in the process of transformation, we may reap discontent. The transformative process - inherent in unavoidable suffering - makes us realize that tragedy often contains the seeds of grace: We can become more than we were before facing the challenges life presented to us. Thus, our humanness unfolds.[15]

Those who are willing and able to be present to others and to accompany them in their process are likely to undergo a transformation as well. Such is the power of altruistic love, of selfless caring; it touches the very soul of the other. It also liberates the giver of such love from the fetters of fear. Death turns into a commonplace matter, and its reign of fear diminishes. As a consequence, life seems cast upon a higher plane. Grace has touched the lives of both, the giver and the receiver of such self-transcending love.

Transformation occurs when spirit, the inner living-selfhood, is touched in the therapeutic relationship, pastoral encounter or genuine friendship. Where there is love — active concern for the well-being and spiritual growth of another — there one can anticipate the mysterious working of *grace* as the silent third partner.

Transformation
The call of death is a call of love.
Death can be sweet if we answer it in the affirmative,
if we accept it as one of the great eternal forms of life and transformation.

(Hermann Hesse)

Notes

1. Ecclesiastes 3:1-2.
2. As told by Irmeli Sjolie of Oslo, Norway, 2005.
3. Henry Coit, M.D., *End of Life Issues*. Lecture Presentation at Medical Conference, San Diego, CA (2006).
4. Hospice information can be obtained at: www.hospicenet.org/ - 20k (1/10/08)
5. Malone: *A Conversation with Viktor Frankl* Public TV station KTEHSA, San Jose, CA (1992).
6. Elisabeth Lukas, *Meaning in Suffering*. Berkeley, CA: Institute of

Logotherapy Press (1986) p. 62.

7   Kok, James R. & Jongsma, A.E., Jr., *The Pastoral Counseling Treatment Planner.* New York: John Wiley & Sons, Inc. (1998), p. 11.

8   Emanuel Swedenborg, *Heaven and Hell* (Dole Translation), West Chester, PA: The Swedenborg Foundation (1985), §411.

9   Viktor E. Frankl, *Man's Search for Ultimate Meaning.* New York: Plenum Press (1997), p. 151. Other major works by Viktor Frankl are: *Man's Search for Meaning,* New York: Washington Square Press (1967/1985); *The Doctor and the Soul,* New York: Vintage Books (1986: revised and expanded edition); *The Will to Meaning,* New York: Meridian (1969/1988).

10 Ewert Cousins, *An Encyclopedic History of the Religious Quest,* as quoted by Ann V. Graber in *Viktor Frankl's Logotherapy: Method of Choice in Ecumenical Pastoral Psychology.* Lima, OH: Wyndham Hall Press (2004), p. 51.

11 Matthew 18:20.

12 Pierre Teilhard de Chardin, *The Future of Man.* New York: Harper Torchbooks (1964), p. 224.

13 Thomas Moore, *Care of the Soul: A Guide for Cultivating Depth and Sacredness in Everyday Life.* New York: HarperCollins Publishers (1992).

14 It is beyond the scope of this paper to elaborate on the clinical stages of the dying process. Detailed descriptions can be found in the book *On Death and Dying* by Elisabeth Kűbler-Ross. New York: Macmillan (1976).

15 John O'Donahue, *Anam Cara – A Book of Celtic Wisdom.* New York: HarperCollins (1997), pp. 199-223.

Poems

Faith by Kahlil Gibran
Life, The Unbelievable by Edwin Markham
Transformation by Herman Hesse

The Beloved Community: Martin Luther King, Jr. and Hope for the City

C. Anthony Hunt

This essay was first delivered as the Martin Luther King, Jr. Lecture at Loyola College in Baltimore, Maryland on January 15, 2007.

This year, we celebrate the 78th anniversary of the birth of Rev. Dr. Martin Luther King, Jr., the African-American Baptist preacher from Georgia who shook the foundations of American society. Dr. King's faith in God is to be viewed as inseparable from the lessons of theology and fellowship that he taught, and the hope of *Beloved Community* that he perpetually sought to convey to all of humanity.

Blinded by parochial assumptions, it seems that too many persons continue to be tempted to reduce and confine the rich complexity of King's thought and praxis to the limits of quotations from a familiar speech. Without seeking to comprehend the depth and breadth of the man – the true measure of his unique spiritual and intellectual giftedness – too many of us tend to find ourselves consistently at the point of simply quoting one of the lines from his famous "I Have a Dream" recitation, delivered in our Nation's Capital in the summer of 1963.

The great 20th century theologian and philosopher Howard Thurman once stated, "Any text without a context is a pretext." It is my observation that our collective attempts to comprehend and appropriate the work of Martin Luther King, Jr. have typically resulted in a pretext. Our attempts to know and relate with King, in historical perspective, have often resulted in too many persons taking his life and work out of context. We know of the "I Have a Dream" speech. We may even know that he was a minister, and some of us may know that he earned a doctor of philosophy degree in Systematic Theology from Boston University in 1955, at a time when the insipid nature of blatant, overt racism – segregation, and Jim/Jane Crow - continued to infect and afflict the United States in both the South and the North.

But too many persons - both white and black - continue to *caricature, canonize, and castigate* King without grappling with the full measure of the man. Too few persons - in the church, the academy, and the general population - have sought to comprehend King and his life and work in full context. Thus, King's life remains a pretext – waiting yet to be fully discovered, uncovered, unpacked, explicated, exegeted, interrogated and ultimately appropriated.

Certainly owing to the eloquence of King's words, it is easy for us to lose sight of his singular vision of *Beloved Community*. At the genesis of a new millennium, I believe that it is critical for us to recall and reclaim the prophetic vision of Martin Luther King, Jr., whose hope for the world led him to stand up against the most dominant and insipid social evils of his day – racism, capitalism (classism) and militarism (war) - what he termed the "triplets of evil". His concerns about the war in Viet Nam were most clearly and eloquently shared in two sermons delivered late in his life: "Declaration of Independence from the War in Vietnam" ("Beyond Vietnam"), delivered at Manhattan's Riverside Church on April 4, 1967, and "A Drum Major Instinct", also delivered in 1967.

In this paper, I will specifically address the issue of *"The Beloved Community"*, with particular focus on what the realization of the prospect of *Beloved Community* might offer with regard to "Hope for the City."

Of particular interest to the contemporary urban context is how the notion of *Beloved Community* might help in the process of re-politicizing, re-socializing, and re-strategizing in the movement toward hope for the city, and how the education of our young might serve as a means toward this end.

The Search for Beloved Community (Beloved Community Defined)

The singular vision of Martin Luther King, Jr. was for the realization of *Beloved Community*. Kenneth Smith and Ira Zepp, Jr., in their seminal 1974 work entitled, *Search for the Beloved Community*, suggest that King's perspective on the Christian love-ethic provides critical insight into understanding his persistent search for the *Beloved Community*. For King, it was rooted in the biblical notion of *Agape* (God's unconditional love), and was the ultimate goal for society.[1]

In King's conception of *Beloved Community*, faith and action were interrelated. In this regard, theology and ethics were inextricably connected. Theology – what we believe and comprehend about God (how we talk about God), could not be separated from ethics – how we behave as the human family. Our creed and our deed have to be in concert. Our talk and our walk have to correspond.

This faith-action (creed-deed) dialectic found its ultimate expression in the notion of *Beloved Community*. For King, there were two steps involved in the movement towards *Beloved Community*. First, *desegregation* would lead to the removal of legal barriers to equality. But desegregation was a short-term goal – and it alone was not enough. Desegregation had to be followed by *integration*. *Integration* advocated and facilitated the inclusion of all persons in a just society. King defined integration as genuine inter-group, interpersonal living. Integration was the long-term goal as a means

toward realizing the vision of *Beloved Community*.
King asserted that "all life is interrelated." One of his fundamental beliefs was in the kinship of all persons. He believed all life is part of a single process; all living things are interrelated; and all persons are sisters and brothers. All have a place in the *Beloved Community*. Because all are interrelated, one cannot harm another without harming oneself. King said:

> To the degree that I harm my brother, no matter what he is doing to me, to that extent I am harming myself. For example, white men often refuse federal aid to education in order to avoid giving the Negro his rights; but because all men are brothers they cannot deny Negro children without harming themselves. Why is this? Because all men are brothers. If you harm me, you harm yourself. Love, *agape*, is the only cement that can hold this broken community together. When I am commanded to love, I am commanded to restore community, to resist injustice, and to meet the needs of my brothers.[2]

The *Beloved Community* was to be an integrated community in which persons of all races and creeds lived together harmoniously as sisters and brothers in peace. It was the Kingdom of God on earth. King stated, "I do not think of political power as an end. Neither do I think of economic power as an end. They are ingredients in the objective we seek in life. And I think that end, that objective, is a truly brotherly society, the creation of *Beloved Community*."[3]

Today, it is in the affirmation of the God-giftedness of all humanity, as manifest in the perpetual striving toward *Beloved Community*, that society can begin to constructively address disintegration and disunity such as racism and its concomitant evils - economic deprivation and military annihilation - that continue to serve as hindrances to true peace and authentic community.

King said, "True peace is not merely the absence of tension – true peace is the presence of justice." King's vision of *Beloved*

Community was rooted in justice. Without justice, there was no possibility of the realization of authentic, peaceful community.

Beloved Community and Hope

King's conception of *Beloved Community* was intricately connected with the notion of hope. For King, Christian hope essentially served as the foundation for his vision of *Beloved Community*. In one of his later sermons, "The Meaning of Hope," he defined hope as that quality which is "necessary for life."[4]

King asserted that hope was to be viewed as "animated and under girded by faith and love." In his mind, if you had hope, you had faith in something. "Hope is generated and animated by love, and is under girded by faith." Thus, hope shares the belief that "all reality hinges on moral foundations."[5]

King intimated that, "the true measure of a person's character is not how one conducts oneself in times of comfort and convenience, but how one conducts oneself in times of challenge and controversy."

"The hopeless individual is the dead individual." In King's view hope has a transformative quality that keeps human beings "alive" both spiritually and psychologically.[6] Hope, therefore, is "one of the basic structures of an adequate life." And so it was that Dr. King would share in the "I Have a Dream" speech his belief that "with this faith, we will be able to hew out of the mountain of despair – the stone of hope."

This hope would seem to serve as a remedy to the nihilism that philosopher Cornel West has often spoken of – where a certain nothingness, meaninglessness, lovelessnesss, and hopelessness seems to have pervaded and permeated so much of our society today – particularly in the urban context. Notice that the backdrop for West's reflections here on nihilism is the Los Angeles riots of April 1992, which followed the acquittal of the police officers charged in the beating of Rodney King.[7]

When the Montgomery Bus Boycott ended, Martin Luther King, Jr. spoke at a victory rally on December 3, 1956. He spoke words of hope for the future. He pointed out that the goal of the boycott had not been to defeat other persons, but to awaken the conscience of others to challenge the false sense of superiority that persons might harbor. Now that victory had been achieved, King said, it was time for reconciliation. "The end is reconciliation; the end is the creation of *Beloved Community.*"

The City as the Context of Martin Luther King, Jr.'s Life and Ministry

It is important to note that the majority of King's life was rooted in the city and much of his work was done within the urban context. Although Lewis V. Baldwin, in *There is a Balm in Gilead,* accurately asserts that King's cultural roots were "folk, black, and southern,"[8] I would add to this that King's roots were also urban.

King's identity was shaped by this southern urban context. According to Baldwin, Atlanta, where King was born and raised, was similar to many southern cities and quite typical of the South, generally. It was not the rural South, but many of its black and white residents had come from rural areas. Atlanta was larger and more industrialized and commercialized than most southern cities, and had more educated, prosperous, and sophisticated people than most southern cities, but many of its residents were illiterate and poverty stricken. The lives of its citizens were dominated by the conventions of Jim Crow, blatantly symbolized in segregated housing, churches, schools, hotels, theatres, restrooms, lunch counters, buses, and centers of recreation.[9]

The Auburn Avenue section on the northeast side of Atlanta, where King was raised, was described in the 1940s as "a quiet Negro business district of decorous hotels and office buildings." According to King, this section comprised blacks of average income who shared a sense of community and spiritual values that created very strong bonds of emotional security.[10]

King was a person of the city. After spending his first 19 years living in Atlanta while attending elementary school through college at Morehouse College, King then traveled north to study at Crozier Theological Seminary, located in Chester, Pennsylvania, just outside of Philadelphia. After graduating from seminary in 1951 at the age of 22, he traveled further north to live and study in another large urban area, while working on his Ph.D. at Boston University.

Reflections on a Doctoral Immersion

I became more acutely aware of Martin Luther King's profound connection to the urban context in August 2006 when I led a doctoral immersion course of Wesley Theological Seminary students and faculty to Birmingham, Montgomery and Selma, Alabama. The course included 22 persons - 18 doctoral students and four faculty members.

The doctoral course in Alabama was entitled "Retracing the Steps of Freedom," and was designed for us to visit and study in some of the more significant settings of the Civil Rights movement.

During the immersion course, we were reminded that many of the major events of the civil rights movement occurred in urban areas. For instance, when King was deciding on where to accept his first pastoral appointment, he decided to accept the appointment to Dexter Avenue Baptist Church in the city of Montgomery, Alabama. He served as the pastor of Dexter Avenue Church from 1954-1960 at the height of the Montgomery Bus Boycott and other significant events. Montgomery is the capital city of the state of Alabama, and it is important to note that just two blocks from Dexter Avenue Church sits the First Confederate White House - the home of Jefferson Davis, the first president of the Confederacy. Sitting between Dexter Avenue Church and the Confederate White House is the Alabama State Capitol – the place where Governor George Wallace and other state officials stood in defiance of any efforts towards integration and equal rights among the races.

King also did considerable work in Birmingham, the city where he wrote the notable Letter from a Birmingham Jail in April 1963. Located in downtown Birmingham is the 16th Street Baptist Church, which on September 15, 1963 was bombed by segregationists, and where four Black girls were killed in the church basement while preparing for their Children's Day worship service. Across the street from 16th Street Church sits Kelly Ingram Park, where many of the protest marches in the city of Birmingham began, and which became notorious for the atrociously violent acts of Police Commissioner Eugene "Bull" Connor and the Birmingham police, as they turned dogs and fire hoses on Black children of Birmingham.

The city of Selma, Alabama was also a significant city during the Civil Rights movement, and a place where King did considerable work. Selma is well-known as the site of "Bloody Sunday", where on March 7, 1965 approximately 600 blacks and some whites gathered in an effort to march across the Edmund Pettus Bridge towards Montgomery to demand voting rights, only to be violently tear-gassed, cattle prodded, bloodily beaten and turned back by state and local authorities.

It is also important to note that King and others spent a considerable amount of time working in cities like Chicago, Washington, DC and Memphis, TN, where King was assassinated on April 4, 1968 while advocating on behalf of sanitation workers of that city.

Hope for the City: King and Education

Martin Luther King viewed education as critical to the movement toward *Beloved Community*, hope and equality. With regard to education and its purpose, Dr. King offered some of his most definitive insight in 1948 at the age of 19 while he was a student at Morehouse College in an essay entitled, "The Purpose of Education."

King pointed out that it seemed to him that "education has a twofold purpose in the life of (humanity) and society: the one is utility and the other is culture." He stated that, "Education must enable (persons) to become more efficient, to achieve with increasing facility the legitimate goals of life."[11]

King went on to share that:

Education must also train (persons) for quick, resolute and effective thinking. To think incisively and to think for one's self is very difficult. We are prone to let our mental life become invaded by legions of half truths, prejudices, and propaganda. At this point, I often wonder whether or not education is fulfilling its purpose. A great majority of the so-called educated people do not think logically and scientifically. Even the press, the classroom, the platform, and the pulpit in many instances do not give us objective and unbiased truths. To save (persons) from the morass of propaganda, in my opinion, is one of the chief aims of education. Education must enable one to sift and weigh evidence, to discern the true from the false, the real from the unreal, and the facts from the fiction.

The function of education, therefore, is to teach one to think intensively and to think critically. But education which stops with efficiency may prove the greatest menace to society. The most dangerous criminal may be the man gifted with reason and no morals.

We must remember that intelligence is not enough. Intelligence plus character – that is the goal of true education. The complete education gives one not only power of concentration, but worthy objectives upon which to concentrate. The broad education will, therefore, transmit to one not only the accumulated knowledge of the race but also the accumulated experience of social living.

If we are not careful, our colleges will produce a group

of closed-minded, unscientific, illogical propagandists, consumed with immoral acts.

Hope for the City: A Look to the Future

Today's cities face any number of issues that present very real challenges to the prospect of the realization of *Beloved Community*. Cities like Baltimore face ongoing issues with escalating poverty and high school dropout rates, increases in violent crime rates, issues related to urban health, unemployment, under-employment, and drug addiction, among many others. Notice that in the first 10 days of 2007, there were 15 persons murdered in the city of Baltimore.

Developing constructive approaches to educating the urban young perhaps presents some of the most critical opportunities for turning the tide on the blight now evident in much of urban life. Why is the education of the young important?

Dietrich Bonhoeffer, the great German Protestant theologian, executed for opposing Hitler's holocaust, said that the test of the morality of a society is how it treats its children.

I believe that Frederick Douglas's statement from more than a century and a half ago sheds additional light on the critical importance of properly educating today's urban young. Douglas intimated that "literacy unfits a child for slavery." I believe that education today, unfits our children for poverty, addiction and imprisonment.

The 2005 "Equality Index," published by the National Urban League sheds more light on the challenges of urban education. It points to significant disparities among urban and suburban educational systems in several areas, including the quality of education (including teacher quality and credentialing), as well as educational attainment/achievement.[12]

According to recent statistics compiled by the national "No Child Left Behind" initiative, the percentage of teachers who are "highly qualified" in their specialty areas is typically higher in the wealthiest school jurisdictions. In the Baltimore-Washington Standard Metropolitan Statistical Area (SMSA) in three of the wealthiest/best-performing school districts: Fairfax County, VA, Montgomery Co., MD and Howard Co., MD, over 90% of teachers are reported to be highly qualified. By comparison, in three of the poorest/worst-performing school districts: the District of Columbia, Prince George's Co., MD and Baltimore City, less than 55% of teachers are reported to be highly qualified.[13]

Several studies point out that differences in academic achievement among Black, Hispanic and White children appear early in the elementary-school years and persist throughout the elementary- and secondary-school years. For instance, Dr. Freeman Hrabowski - president of the University of Maryland, Baltimore County - and his collaborators in the book, *Beating the Odds: Raising Academically Successful African American Males*, point out that a report on the performance of elementary school children in Montgomery County, Maryland shows that the percentage of Hispanic and Black children who fell behind their White peers in mathematics increased markedly between the first and sixth grades. At the second grade, more than 15% of Black and Hispanic children and approximately 5% of the White children were performing below grade level. By the sixth grade, the performance of 20 % of White children, while the performance of over 40% of the Hispanic and 50% of the Black children, was below grade level.[14]

It is also important to note that many Black and Hispanic children live in urban settings where school systems receive far less funding per student than their suburban counterparts. The difference in funding, for example, for students in the city of Baltimore and Montgomery County, one of the wealthiest counties in the country is almost $2,000 per student per year.

It is important that we give constructive attention to how children in urban areas are being educated because – as Marian Wright Edelman of the Children's Defense Fund points out - urban children of any race face the higher likelihood of being abused and neglected, born into poverty, born without health insurance, killed by a firearm, or born to a teenage mother. These figures are exacerbated for black and brown children. An African American or Hispanic preschool boy born in 2001 has about a one-in-three chance of going to prison in his lifetime. Black and brown girls represent the fastest growing group of detained juveniles. Black and brown youth are 48 times more likely to be incarcerated than white youth for comparable drug offenses.[15]

It is important that we give careful attention to constructive, creative approaches to educating children in urban areas in light of the observation of Paul Vallas – the chief executive of the Philadelphia Public School System – in 2002. Vallas offered that those who are doing projections on the future need for prison cells in the burgeoning prison-industrial complex in America are basing their projections on the academic performance and achievement of fourth grade African-American and Latino boys today. To shed light on the expansion of the prison industrial complex in America, Professor Lani Guinier recently pointed out that in California, an entry level prison guard with a high school diploma can expect to make a starting salary of about $51,000.00, while a new assistant professor in the University of California system with a Ph.D. can expect to earn a starting salary of about $31,000.00.

Is There a Balm? Final Thoughts on Beloved Community and Hope for the City

In the final analysis, Martin Luther King, Jr. was a preacher-theologian, and his hope for humanity, his hope for the city, his hope for every neighborhood and every hamlet, his hope for every child, black, white, brown and yellow, was rooted in a biblical faith. This was a faith nurtured in the city of Atlanta. This was a faith that went with him to some of the great cities of this nation and world.

It was a faith shaped by the Sermon on the Mount, and the ethical teachings of Christ (Matthew 5-7). It was a faith that would drive his persistent hope for the realization of *Beloved Community*.

For King, hope was the refusal to give up "despite overwhelming odds." This is a hope that would beckon us to love everybody – both our enemies and allies. This is a hope that would help us to see that we can resist giving up on one another because our lives together are animated by the doctrine of *imago dei* – and that God is present in each and every one of us.

Is There a Balm?

> "Is there no balm in Gilead; is there no physician there? Why then has the health of my poor people not been restored?" (Jeremiah 8:22)

These questions, posed by the Prophet Jeremiah in Jeremiah chapter 8, were asked in the 7th century B.C.E. in light of the experience of exile and pain for the people of Israel. The region of Gilead was known for producing a healing balm. This balm was known for its medicinal powers. When people were hurting, they would seek out the balm from Gilead, for it was like no other in its ability to facilitate healing. The balm from Gilead was considered to be a miracle cure, and if it couldn't heal one's wounds, there was perhaps nothing that would.

Jeremiah was speaking to the Israelites, who found themselves dealing with brokenness and alienation from God, brokenness and alienation from their land, brokenness and alienation from their possessions, and brokenness and alienation from one another.

> "Is there no balm in Gilead; is there no physician there? Why then has the health of my poor people not been restored?"

On numerous occasions, Martin Luther King, Jr. pointed out that the nature of hope is evident in these questions posed by the prophet – and is embodied in the Black faith experience in America. These questions shaped much of the public faith and life of Dr. Martin Luther King, Jr., and have shaped the life of the black Christian community for more than three centuries. It is important to re-visit these questions of faith relative to the city today, for to pose such questions helps us to define and shape our life and future together.

There is a Balm

King intimated that amidst the oppression that they had experienced in slavery, and jim- and jane-crow segregation – African-American Christians were able to convert the *question marks* of the prophet Jeremiah's lament, into an *exclamation point* as they affirmed their faith and hope in the living and life-giving God:

> There is a balm in Gilead,
> to make the wounded whole
> There is a balm in Gilead,
> To heal the sin-sick soul
> Sometimes I feel discouraged
> And think my work's in vain
> And then the Holy Spirit
> Revives my soul again![16]

There's hope for the city. With faith in God, I am convinced that we will be able, as Dr. King dreamed, "to hew out of the mountain of despair, a stone of hope." Finally, Dr. King shared that everybody can be great because everybody can serve. He further shared that our service is the rent that we pay for the space that we occupy here on earth. Let us be hopeful that each of those who around this nation and the globe celebrate Dr. King's life will be committed to paying some rent.

Notes

1 Kenneth Smith and Ira Zepp, Jr., *Search for the Beloved Community* (Valley Forge, PA: Judson Press), see pp. 129-156.

2 Martin Luther King, Jr., "Loving Your Enemies," *Strength to Love* (New York: York: Harper, 1963), pp. 41-50.

3 Martin Luther King, Jr., "Suffering and Faith" in *The Christian Century* (Chicago, IL: Christian Century, July 13, 1966).

4 King, sermon delivered on December 10, 1967, see Garth Baker-Fletcher, *Somebodyness: Martin Luther King, Jr. and the Theory of Dignity*, (Minneapolis, MN: Fortress Press, 1993), 132.

5 Baker-Fletcher, 132.

6 Ibid.

7 Cornel West, *Race Matters* (Boston: Beacon Press, 1993), 11-20.

8 Lewis V. Baldwin, *There is a Balm in Gilead: The Cultural Roots of Martin Luther King, Jr.* (Minneapolis: Fortress Press, 1991), 3.

9 Ibid., 17.

10 Martin Luther King, Jr., "An Autobiography of Religious Development," (1950), see Clayborne Carson, ed., *The Papers of Martin Luther King, Jr.*, Volume 1: *Called to Serve*, (Berkley, CA: University of California Press, 1992), 359.

11 King, "The Purpose of Education," (1948) (www.toptags.com/aama/voices/speeches/pofed.htm, see also Clayborne Carson, ed., *The Papers of Martin Luther King, Jr.*, Volume 1: *Called to Serve* (Berkley, CA: University of California Press, 1992), 122.

12 National Urban League, *The State of Black America-2006: The Opportunity Compact* (New York: National Urban League, 2006), p. 133 f.

13 see *The Washington Post*, January 13, 2007

14 Freeman Hrabowski,, III, et. al., *Beating the Odds: Raising Academically Successful African American Males* (Oxford, UK: Oxford University Press, 1998).

15 National Urban League, *The State of Black America-2006: The Opportunity Compact*, p. 133 f.

16 See *Songs of Zion* (Nashville: Abingdon Press, 1974), 123.

Suggested Reading

Baker-Fletcher, Garth. *Somebodyness: Martin Luther King, Jr. and the Theory of Dignity.* Minneapolis, MN: Fortress Press, 1993.

Baldwin, Lewis V. *There is a Balm in Gilead: The Cultural Roots of Martin Luther King, Jr.* Minneapolis: Fortress Press, 1991.

Baldwin, Lewis V. *To Make the Wounded Whole: The Cultural Legacy of Martin Luther King, Jr.* Minneapolis: Fortress Press, 1993.

Franklin, Robert M. *Liberating Visions: Human Fulfillment and Social Justice in African American Thought.* Minneapolis: Fortress Press, 1990.

Hrabowski, Freeman, III, et. al. *Beating the Odds: Raising Academically Successful African American Males.* Oxford, UK: Oxford University Press, 1998.

Hrabowski, Freeman, III, et. al. *Overcoming the Odds: Raising Academically Successful African American Young Females.* Oxford, UK: Oxford University Press, 2002.

Hunt, C. Anthony. *And Yet the Melody Lingers: Essays, Sermons and Prayers on Religion and Race.* Lima, OH: Wyndham Hall Press, 2006.

Hunt, C. Anthony. *Blessed are the Peacemakers: A Theological Analysis of the Thought of Howard Thurman and Martin Luther King, Jr.* Lima, OH: Wyndham Hall Press, 2005.

Hunt, C. Anthony. *Upon the Rock: A Model for Ministry with Black Families.* Lima, OH: Wyndham Hall Press, 2001.

Hunt, C. Anthony. "Martin Luther King, Jr.: Resistance, Nonviolence and Community" in *Black Leaders and Ideologies in the South: Resistance and Nonviolence*, Preston King and Walter Earl Fluker, eds. London, UK: Critical Review of Social and Political Philosophy, 2004.

King, Martin Luther, Jr. *Strength to Love.* New York: Harper, 1963.

King, Martin Luther, Jr. "The Purpose of Education," (www.toptags.com/aama/voices/speeches/pofed.htm), 1948.

National Urban League. *2005 Equality Index.* New York: National Urban League, 2005.

National Urban League. *The State of Black America, 2006: The Opportunity Compact.* New York: National Urban League, 2006.

Smith, Kenneth and Ira Zepp, Jr. *Search for the Beloved Community.* Valley Forge, PA: Judson Press, 1974.

Watley, William D. *Roots of Resistance: The Nonviolent Ethic of Martin Luther King, Jr.* Valley Forge, PA: Judson Press, 1985.

West, Cornel. *Race Matters.* Boston: Beacon Press, 1993.

The Moral Responsibility of Leadership in Tenuous Times: A Higher Imperative
Paul J. Kirbas

In his classic 1947 book *The History of Western Philosophy,* the famous author and future Nobel Prize winner Bertrand Russell devoted a large section of his work to the period of time commonly known as "The Dark Ages". This period of time, which Russell brackets between 600 AD and 1000 AD (although others extend the period), is marked by tremendous instability, religious conflict, and terrible crimes against humanity by some that Russell generally identifies as "the Barbarians". Indeed, even to this day, the phrase "that's barbarian" is used to describe behavior far outside the norm in its violation of civil codes. As Russell charts his account of history up to the eve of this period, he recognizes that it is preceded by a very tenuous time, in which western culture might have been steered into a different direction and therefore avoided the "dark ages" altogether. That course, however, failed to materialize. In a brief moment of personal commentary within his historical accounting, Russell posits the placement of blame for this failed opportunity. The blame does not rest with "the barbarians" or with the Roman officials. For Russell, the blame is placed on the doorstep of the Church, and particularly the leadership of the Church. Russell writes:

> It is strange that the last men of intellectual eminence before the dark ages were concerned, not with saving civilization or expelling the barbarians or reforming the abuses of the administration, but with preaching the merit of virginity and the damnation of un-baptized infants. Seeing that these were the preoccupations that the Church handed on to the converted barbarians, it is no wonder that the succeeding age surpassed almost all other fully historical periods in cruelty and superstition.[1]

In this quote, Bertrand Russell raises some important issues about the responsibility of Church leaders in the use and application of theology. For Russell, theological principles can not exist in a vacuum. They will, rather, dynamically interact with the environment in which they are offered. The "last men of intellectual eminence" in Russell's statement failed to take the larger social context into account as they offered their theological pronouncements. In doing this, they contributed to the downfall of the western world in two ways. First, they failed to constructively contribute to the betterment of society, or to what Russell called the act of "saving civilization". Surely these leaders could have used their authority to help the larger society to move into a more positive direction. Within the corpus of theological dogma, they could have chosen agendas and championed causes that led their new barbarian leaders to embrace a more grace-filled Christianity. If they chose this path, perhaps today the phrase "that's barbarian" would be a compliment saved for the nicest acts of Christian care.

There is, however, a second way in which the church leaders addressed by Bertrand Russell failed in their moral responsibility of leadership. Not only did they fail to constructively contribute to the betterment of society, but they actually, albeit unintentionally, contributed to the most "barbaric" acts of the barbarians. By choosing to preserve dogmas such as the damnation of un-baptized infants, for instance, these leaders created a Christian worldview in which some human life was seen as lacking the sanctity that human life deserves. For Russell, this created a theological environment that encouraged inhumane treatment, the kind of which became legendary for the barbarians.

These two results that stem from the choices that certain Church leaders made concerning the particular dogmas that they would champion led to the charge of failed moral leadership in Russell's classic work. For Russell, these leaders may have won some points for their own sense of preserving dusty dogmas, but they lost the larger goal of offering positive and constructive leadership in a tenuous time. There is a moral responsibility of leadership in such times, and that moral responsibility is a higher imperative than preserving dogma.

Beyond Bertrand

The example above illustrates the belief that theology is a social enterprise, and those who engage in the work of theology have a moral responsibility to take the social context into consideration as they offer theological expression and reflection. Bertrand Russell makes a good point, but clearly a point from "below". He was a philosopher, and never suggested that he was speaking for God. In fact, one of Russell's later writings was his 1957 book, *Why I Am Not a Christian*. Although he raises a good starting point, one must ask why theologically inclined thinkers should pay any heed. Do we find any collaboration, from Scripture, the early church, basic theologies, or respected theist philosophers, that supports the view that social context provides a moral imperative for the expression of theology? A short essay can not do justice to this question, but we can tease out some answers for illustrative purposes. The reader is invited to delve deeper into these examples, to see if the points hold true.

There is, in fact, supportive evidence in the Hebrew Scriptures that social context provides a higher moral responsibility than the preservation of dogma. The Hebrew Scriptures reveal a tension between the passion of God toward social healing and the pious expressions of faith offered by those who fail to recognize their higher moral responsibility. A classic example is found in Amos 5:21-24:

> I hate, I despise your religious feasts; I cannot stand your assemblies. Even though you bring me burnt offerings and grain offerings, I will not accept them. Though you bring choice fellowship offerings, I will have no regard for them. Away with the noise of your songs! I will not listen to the music of your harps. But let justice roll on like a river, righteousness like a never-failing stream![2]

Although this is but one example, it is far from being an isolated one. Throughout the Hebrew Scriptures, there is a constant tension between mere lip expression of faith and dogma, without an awareness of the urgent social context surrounding that expression. The needs of that social context seem to trump any isolated allegiance to dogma. Dr. Walter Brueggemann, a leading authority on the studies of the Hebrew Scriptures, states:

> My thesis is this: In the face of the rich pluralism and passionate interestedness of the biblical text in its various local voices, the text everywhere is concerned with the costly reality of human hurt and the promised alternation of evangelical hope.[3]

There is also a similar cord found in the New Testament, and in the ministry of Jesus Christ. Much of the Gospels' material presents the conflict between Jesus and the Pharisees. The Pharisees are the preservers of Dogma, whereas Jesus always sees a higher moral responsibility resting within the social context. Many times this contest is evident in the Pharisaic dogma concerning the Sabbath, and Jesus' repeated breaking of it in response to the social context around him.

As we turn to the early church, we see that St. Augustine would have no problem finding truth in the words of Bertrand Russell, for he advocated for the existence of truth in non-theistic philosophy. "Usually even a non-Christian knows something about the Earth, the heavens, and the other elements of this world and this knowledge he holds to as being certain from reason and experience," Augustine stated.[4] Augustine also passionately expressed his belief that one will find God, and God's true will, within the social context of relatedness rather than in written dogmas. Augustine writes:

> "God is love." Why should we go speeding to the height of heaven and the nethermost parts of the earth, seeking for him who is with us, if we would but be with him? Let none say: "I do not know what I am to love." Let him love his brother, and he will love that same love: He knows the love whereby he loves better than the brother whom he loves. God can be more known to him than his brother—really more known because more present; more known because more inward; more known because more sure. Embrace the love that is God: through love embrace God. He is the very love that links together in holy bond all good angels and all God's servants, and unites them and us to one another and in obedience to himself. The more we are clean from the cancer of pride, the more we are filled with love; and he who is filled with love is filled with God.[5]

The above quote comes from a larger teaching of Augustine on the subject of the Trinity, and the very doctrine of the Trinity offers theological support for seeing theology as necessarily connected to the social context. Although this historical church doctrine remains shrouded in mystery, one commonly held belief is that it reveals to us that God is, in essence, a *relationship*. God can not exist apart from relationship. Therefore, theology (the study of God) is bound up in the dynamics of relationship. One can not possibly discover God in isolation, for God does not exist in isolation. God is a social being, and theology must be a social enterprise.

Although he wasn't promoting the doctrine of the Trinity, the famous Jewish philosopher Martin Buber offered a compelling case for seeing the essentiality of relationship at all levels in his classic book *I and Thou*. For Buber, no one, not even God, can exist without existing *in relationship*. Once again, the social context of relatedness trumps the isolated existence of dogma.

This essay began with a statement from Bertrand Russell, in which he offered an indictment upon the religious leaders of the tenuous time just before the western world collapsed into the dark ages. Those leaders had a moral responsibility to lead culture into a more enlightened future. They also had their own dogmas, handed down from generations past. For Russell, the moral responsibility of leadership in that tenuous time presented a higher imperative than the preaching of authoritative dogma. They failed in their moral responsibility of leadership.

From a variety of accepted sources of insight, including the Hebrew and Christian Scriptures, St. Augustine, the Doctrine of the Trinity, and the work of philosopher Martin Buber, one can find substantive support for Russell's views. Theological dogma can not exist in a vacuum. It always exists within a social context. The dogma can either serve as a source of grace for that social context, or it can exacerbate existing dangers and fragilities. In tenuous times, it becomes the moral responsibility of leaders to understand the social impact of their use of dogma and their choice of its expression, and to ensure that their words work toward the betterment of the social context. To promote dogma that fails to heal a tenuous time, or that contributes to its worsening, is a failure of moral leadership.

In 2008, we are living in such a tenuous time. Recent actions and pronouncements of Pope Benedict XVI may be seen as the preservation of dogma, but may also be evaluated by future *Bertrand Russell's* as a tragic failure of moral leadership.

Pope Benedict XVI

It is not the case that Pope Benedict has changed direction now that he is Pope. To be fair and honest, one must state that he has been very consistent in his thoughts and beliefs. In preparation for this essay, I read through many biographies and books about the Pope, including *Benedict XVI: Commander of the Faith*, by Rupert Shortt, *Benedict XVI: The Man who was Ratzinger*, by Michael Rose, *Pope Benedict XVI: A personal Portrait*, by H.J. Fischer, and *The Thoughts of Benedict XVI*, by Aidan Nichols. In all these sources, Pope Benedict has been presented as a strong defender of traditional Catholic doctrine. The sources depict him as the voice of caution at the Second Vatican Council. Some suggest (i.e. Shortt) that as the Prefect to Pope John Paul II, Ratzinger exercised his influence to limit Pope John Paul's enactment of Vatican II. In other words, Pope John Paul II was far more of a reformer at heart than what his actual papacy indicated, but his reforming tendencies were mitigated largely due to the influence of Ratzinger.

In a hopeful book published shortly before the death of Pope John Paul II entitled *Is the Reformation Over?*, the Wheaton College professor (now at Notre Dame) Mark Noll lauded the ecumenical actions of Pope John Paul II, and envisioned a new era of Protestant-Catholic relationships. Perhaps what Mark Noll should have been paying attention to was the writings of Prefect Cardinal Joseph Ratzinger. In the year 2000, Ratzinger wrote a declaration entitled *"Dominus IESUS": On the Unicity and Salvific Universality of Jesus Christ and the Church*. In this document, Ratzinger made it clear that there was but one way to experience salvation, and that was through Jesus Christ. Further, there is but one way to a full relationship with Jesus Christ, and that is through the Roman Catholic Church. Ratzinger strongly opposed what he saw as the "relativistic mentality"[6] that many hold concerning ecumenical relationships within the Christian faith, as well as in inter-religious dialogue. His brush swept across many faiths, including Jews, Muslims, and Protestant Christians. Of this last group, the document stated that "the ecclesial communities which have not preserved the valid Episcopate and the genuine and integral substance of the Eucharistic mystery are not Churches in the proper sense."7

Having stated that as Prefect in 2000, it should not be surprising to hear the now Pope Benedict XVI reiterate the point in 2007. Apparently, Pope Benedict thought that there needed to be some clarifications on certain church matters. In June of 2007, the Vatican published a statement entitled, "Responses to Some Questions Regarding Certain Aspects of the Doctrine of the Church." In this document, Pope Benedict reasserted his view that Protestant churches "cannot, according to Catholic Doctrine, be called 'Churches' in the proper sense."

In the same summer, Pope Benedict lifted restrictions on the use of an ancient Latin Mass known as the *Tridentine Mass*. This action angered many Jewish groups, due to the fact that the mass articulates a hope to convert Jews to Christianity. Offended Protestants and Jews had to stand in line, however. Pope Benedict had already aroused the anger of many Muslim groups. In a speech given in September of 2006, Pope Benedict quoted a 13th century writing that stated:

> Show me just what Muhammad brought that was new and there you will find things only evil and inhuman, such as his command to spread by the sword the faith he preached.8

Pope Benedict quickly clarified his use of this quote, and publicly apologized for the offense that it caused. Perhaps in that moment, the Pope recognized the weapon of words, and the deep responsibility of choosing words carefully when one holds such a powerful position of leadership. The hope of this author would be that the Pope would more deeply reflect on the insight of that moment, and lift its truth to a higher level. The quote was a given. It was in the historical record. The choice to lift up that quote, and to give it life in the modern context, was an error in judgment and in leadership. One may not be able to debate the quote's existence, but one could certainly question why someone in the Pope's position of leadership would choose to invoke it in the particular tenuous time of Christian-Islamic relationships. The moral responsibility of leadership in a tenuous time requires more than just facts, dogma and principle. It requires a grace-filled sensitivity to the social context in which one operates.

Our Tenuous Time

Although Bertrand Russell believed that the Dark Ages "surpassed almost all other fully historical periods in cruelty and superstition", he had not been privy to the particular set of dynamics and issues that face us in the 21st century. Similar to the Dark Ages, our time is marked by a growing ideological divide that carries the potential of violent outbreaks. The new element, however, is the sheer power of our weaponry, and the ability for weapons of mass destruction to fall into the wrong hands. More and more, the potential havoc caused by extremists in our world is becoming a real and present danger. Although the presence of the extremists is relatively small in relationship to the larger human community, they seem to be setting the agenda for the rest of us. Fear and suspicion are grabbing hold of people, and these emotions express themselves in the presence of anyone who is part of the "other" group. Muslims, for instance, are immediately and unwarrantedly viewed with suspicion by many American Christians. Given our present reality, one could imagine two possible scenarios for our future. One possibility is that those who want to create a peaceful and hope-filled world will band together, from all faiths, from all continents, from all political affiliations, and that through the power of a global majority we could create a peaceful and secure future. The other possibility, however, is that fear and suspicion will deepen and spread, and the lines of demarcation between peoples and groups will become stronger. We are, in other words, living in a very tenuous time. It is highly possible that we are in the eve of another kind of "dark ages" period in the history of the human community.

Given this reality, our time is very much like the environment that Bertrand Russell described in the opening quote of this essay. It seems evident, then, that those in positions of Church leadership have a particular moral responsibility, and that this responsibility is a higher imperative than the defense of doctrine and dogma. The higher moral responsibility is to the social context of the day. What does our social context require? It requires the building of bridges between people of difference, the removal of walls that separate people from each other, the diminishment of fear and suspicion, and the unifying of a new global majority in order to combat the growing tides of hostility. Unfortunately, the statements and actions of Pope Benedict XVI have made it clear that the Pope is not offering this kind of leadership. Given the particularly tenuous times in which we live, his legacy may be evaluated by future historians as the Pope who won the day for dogma, but in the end, failed to offer the moral leadership needed.

Conclusion

My assignment for this essay was to write a Protestant response to the recent statements of the Pope concerning Protestant churches. My first thought was to try to mount a theological defense for Protestant authenticity. It quickly seemed apparent, however, that this would be fruitless. In the end, Pope Benedict XVI has the right to believe what he does, and it is even admirable that he is unwilling to compromise his beliefs for political purposes. As a Protestant, I can not stand outside his theological tradition and tear down the fabric of his doctrine and his dogma.

Yet even if that dogma is a real and historical given, Pope Benedict XVI is exercising his own freedoms in choosing the dogmas that he champions, and it is in this freedom that his moral responsibility comes in focus. Just as the dogma of the Sabbath was made subservient to the social needs that Jesus encountered, so too the dogmas of the Catholic Church that promote hostility, suspicion, and division within the larger human community should remain subservient to the particular needs of our social context. At his September 2006 speech, it would have been better if Pope Benedict hadn't invoked that 13th century quote that angered Muslims. In his June 2007 proclamation, it would have been better if he had not re-emphasized his view on Protestants. In his July 2007 revival of the Tridentine Mass, it would have been better if he hadn't allowed the liturgy concerning the conversion of the Jews to resurface in our modern times. Within the rich resources of Catholic theology, there are so many other themes to champion. There would be no trouble finding the themes that promote love, peace, and justice. Let us hope that Pope Benedict finds those themes, and begins to use his place of authority and influence to help move our world away from the brink of disaster; for that is the leadership we need in such a time as this.

Let us hope that Pope Benedict XVI discovers the higher imperative of the moral responsibility of leadership in tenuous times. It is not too late for him to create a better legacy for himself, and a better world for everyone.

Notes

1 Russell, Bertrand. *The History of Western Philosophy.* New York: Simon and Schuster, 1945. p. 366

2 The New International Version of the Bible

3 Brueggemann, Walter. *Old Testament Theology. Essays on Structure, Theme, and Text.*, p. 84

4 St. Augustine in *De Genesi ad litteram libri duodecim*

5   Burnaby, John. (ED) *Augustine: Later Works*, p. 52

6   Ratzinger, *Dominus IESUS*, I.5

7   Ibid, IV.17

8   The passage originally appeared in the "*Dialogue Held With A Certain Persian, the Worthy Mouterizes, in Anakara of Galatia*", written in 1391 as an expression of the views of the Byzantine emperor Manuel Paleologus

Bibliography

Fischer, H.J. *Pope Benedict XVI. A Personal Portrait*. New York: Crossroad Publishing Co., 2005

Nichols, Aidan. *The Thought of Benedict XVI. An Introduction to the Theology of Joseph Ratzinger.* New York: Burns and Oats, 2005.

Noll, Mark A. *Is the Reformation Over? An Evangelical Assessment of Contemporary Roman Catholicism.* Grand Rapids, MI: Baker Academic, 2005

Rose, Michael S. *Benedict XVI. The Man who was Ratzinger.* Dallas: Spence Publishing Co., 2005

Russell, Bertrand. *The History of Western Philosophy.* New York: Simon and Schuster, 1945

Shortt, Rupert. Benedict XVI. *Commander of the Faith.* London: Hodder and Stoughton, 2005

Animal Experiments: Ethics, Theology, and the Possibility of Dialogue

Andrew Linzey

I

There has been considerable public controversy over the use of animals in experimentation at Oxford. The controversy has involved both town and gown. Individuals have taken public stands for and against. There have been heated exchanges, protests, and much acrimonious discourse.

I am referring to the controversy that raged in the last years of the nineteenth century. For example: John Ruskin, the Slade Professor of Fine Art, resigned his post "following the vote endowing vivisection in the University" in 1885.[1] Previously, Lewis Carroll circulated his own anti-vivisection tract entitled *Some Popular Fallacies about Vivisection* in 1875.[2] Frances Power Cobbe, a long time associate of Manchester College (as it then was), launched the Society for the Protection of Animals Liable to Vivisection in the same year.[3] And E. B. Nicholson, Bodley's Librarian no less, wrote the pioneering work *The Rights of an Animal* in 1879.[4]

Reference to this history only serves to emphasise that controversy about animals, and especially animal experimentation, is not new. Indeed, Oxford has been the home of such controversy. One hundred years later, in the 1970s, Peter Singer penned his

Animal Liberation[5] whilst teaching philosophy at University College; Stephen R. L. Clark started his *The Moral Status of Animals*[6] while a Fellow of All Souls, and it was three enterprising philosophy graduates from New College, Balliol and St Hilda's who helped re-start it all by producing the landmark book *Animals, Men and Morals*[7] in 1971 – a work that Singer himself properly described as "the Bible" of the movement.[8] Even my own first little book on *Animal Rights: A Christian Assessment* was published in 1976.[9] Controversy about animals? In truth, we have been growing it in Oxford for decades.

And it is important to recognise that the controversy concerns some hardcore, largely unresolved, questions. Can scientific research exist without causing suffering to animals? Why should animals always bear the cost? And how rightly should we understand ourselves, and evaluate our needs, in relation to the rest of creation? But one most centrally: Is the deliberate infliction of suffering on animals itself ever morally licit?

II

For some of my contemporaries, it is a comparatively small thing to justify the infliction of suffering. "Animals", they say, "are only animals". But that dismissive line obscures the fact that animals suffer only to a greater or lesser extent than we do. There is now ample evidence in peer reviewed scientific journals that all mammals (at least) suffer not just pain, but also shock, fear, terror, anticipation, foreboding, stress, anxiety, and trauma.[10]

If it is true that animals can suffer in these ways which were once considered uniquely human, then it is peculiarly difficult – philosophically - to justify the deliberate infliction of suffering on animals. In addition, there are considerations here that are specifically relevant to animals, as well as some weaker humans, but they seldom receive the attention they should:

Consider: animals cannot give or withhold their consent.

Informed voluntary consent is now regarded as essential in order to justify experimentation on human subjects, but when it comes to animals that relevant factor is always absent. Consider also: animals cannot represent or vocalise their own interests. Individuals who cannot adequately represent themselves have to depend upon others to do so. Unlike even children or the elderly who suffer from dementia, but who can be represented in a court of law, animals seldom have a spokesperson who has "legal standing" (the expression used in the US) who can represent their interests, so it is precisely because they cannot articulate their needs or represent their interests, that these needs are almost always ignored and yet they should invoke a heightened sense of obligation.

Consider further: animals are morally innocent or blameless. Because they are not moral agents with free will, they cannot – strictly speaking – be regarded as morally responsible. As C. S. Lewis rightly observed: "So far as we know beasts are incapable of sin or virtue; therefore they can neither deserve pain nor be improved by it".[11] Consider lastly: animals are vulnerable and defenceless. They are almost wholly within our power and subject to our will. Except in rare circumstances, animals pose us no threat, constitute no risk to our life, and possess no means of offence or defence. Moral solicitude should properly relate to, and be commensurate with, the relative vulnerability of the subject concerned, or what might be termed "ontologies of vulnerability".[12]

The point is that these considerations, when impartially judged (or at least as impartially as humans can manage) mean that the infliction of suffering upon animals is harder, not easier, to justify. Non-consenting, inarticulate, innocent, and vulnerable beings deserve special moral solicitude.[13]

III

Now some people believe that theology can be drawn upon to justify the infliction of suffering. Theology has been central, at least historically, in providing some of the key justifications for the use of animals. But how convincing are they?

"We have dominion over animals", it is often said. I never cease to be amazed at the number of atheists who believe that humans have dominion. For centuries, it needs to be admitted, Christians have interpreted Genesis 1 as meaning little more than "might is right" – a view that has influenced the largely secular view of animals today. But modern scholarship has made clear how wrong we were. The priestly theology of Genesis is not that of man-the-despot, but rather of humanity as the species commissioned to care, under God, for the creation. And in case this appears like liberal revisionism of an ancient text, there is internal evidence in the text itself. In Genesis 1. 26-9, humans are made in God's image and given dominion, and in the subsequent verse (29-30) given a vegetarian diet. Herb-eating dominion is hardly a license for tyranny.

"We humans are made in the image of God", it is often said. But the God in whose image we are made is a God of love, mercy, justice. It is difficult to see how being made in that image can justify the infliction of pain, whatever the motives. Indeed modern scholarship reveals that "image" and "dominion" go together: Humans are to represent God's own benevolent care for other creatures. If one truly believes that God is benevolent and that humans are made in God's image, then our obligations are clear: We also must be benevolent, not just to other humans but to the whole of God's creation. Humans are uniquely responsible to God for how they exercise their authority. The picture that emerges is of a God that creates humans with God-given capacities to care for creation as God's own representative on earth. We are to be not so much the "master species" as the "servant species".[14]

"Only humans have souls, however". In fact, Catholic theology has never denied that animals have souls, only that they possess rational and therefore immortal souls. Quite how that position squares with the biblical vision of the redemption of all creation is for others to judge.[15] But, even if true, the absence of a soul – as C. S. Lewis once indicated - makes the infliction of pain harder to justify:

> For it means that animals cannot deserve pain, nor profit morally by the discipline of pain, nor be recompensed by happiness in another life for suffering in this. Thus, all the factors which render pain more tolerable or make it less totally evil in the case of human beings will be lacking in the beasts. "Soullessness", in so far as it is relevant to the question at all, is an argument against vivisection.[16]

"But humans are rational", we are told, "our lives therefore have a richness and a depth unavailable to other creatures". There are reasons for being wary of the "my life is richer than yours" kind of argument, if only because scientists are increasingly finding ways in which the lives of animals display characteristics and abilities that make us marvel. But even if true, does rationality make our suffering always more significant? While it is possible, for example, that anticipation of death may make humans more liable to suffering, it is also the case that intellectual incomprehension may make the experience of suffering worse. Consider, for example, the predicament of captive animals who have no means of rationalising their deprivation, boredom, and frustration. They have no intellectual means of escaping their circumstances, for example (as far as we can tell) by use of their imagination. They cannot, like Terry Waite in captivity, intellectually appreciate the forces that led to their capture and begin, as he did, to write "in my imagination".[17] It is unclear that rational incomprehension always (to say the least) makes suffering less acute.

"Nevertheless, humans are unique and superior", it is claimed. "We have reason, free will, and we are morally accountable in a way in which animals can never be". But it follows that is precisely because we have those exalted capacities that we should acknowledge duties to them that they cannot acknowledge towards us. Properly understood, moral superiority can never be the basis for behaving in a morally inferior way. And here we reach the decisive consideration from a theological perspective: our power or lordship over animals needs to be related to that exercise of lordship seen in the life of Jesus Christ.

Jesus provides us with what I have called a "paradigm of inclusive moral generosity" that privileges the weak, the vulnerable, the poor, the marginalised, and the outcast. But if costly generosity really is the God-given paradigm then it ought also be the paradigm for the exercise of human dominion over the animal world. The doctrine of the incarnation involves the sacrifice of the "higher" for the "lower", not the reverse. And if that is the true model of divine generosity, it is difficult to see how humans can otherwise interpret their exercise of power over other sentient creatures. As I have written elsewhere:

> When we speak of human superiority, we speak of such a thing properly only and in so far as we speak not only of Christlike lordship but also of Christlike service. There can be no lordship without service and no service without lordship. Our special value in creation consists in being of special value to others.[18]

Now some will say that this discourse wilfully neglects what they see as the central issue: isn't such suffering nevertheless justifiable if it serves laudable ends? Important, serious ends, like the accumulation of scientific knowledge that may help cure disease or alleviate suffering?

But a yes to that question is only readily available to those who hold to a simple kind of utilitarian philosophy, and believe (as I do not) that the ends always justify the means. If I did believe that, I would not want to stop at animals, however. If benefits can justify the infliction of suffering on animals, they should also logically justify the use of weaker human subjects. After all, the results would be more applicable, more certain. That this is the case is recognised even by those who fully support animal experimentation. The philosopher, Raymond Frey writes that, "… we cannot, with the appeal to benefit, justify (painful) animal experiments without justifying (painful) human experiments".[19] That we do not (usually) justify painful experiments on humans without their permission shows precisely what our ethics includes and where it stops, and yet this "boundary line" is arbitrary.

"But we have to experiment on animals because we can't experiment on humans", it is claimed. In fact, animal experimentation has not prevented experimentation on humans: *alongside* the use of animals, vulnerable human subjects such as: children, prisoners of war, Jews, people of colour, the mentally challenged, even ordinary soldiers have been used in experimentation without their knowledge or informed consent or both.[20] And some of us are still disturbed that experiments on human embryos are permissible up to 14 days – to which we shall shortly have to add the phenomenon of animal-human hybrids.[21] To those who once claimed that we must choose between "your dog or your baby", we need to remind ourselves of the counter-claim made by early anti-vivisectionists: it is not a choice between "your dog or your baby" but rather "your dog *and* your baby. It is not a question of animals or human beings, but one of animals *and* human beings".[22]

The foregoing has sketched some of the grounds for regarding the infliction of suffering on non-consenting, inarticulate, innocent, and vulnerable creatures as intrinsically wrong. I am always rather bemused when people talk about "emotional arguments" for animals, when in truth the purely rational case is one of the strongest in ethics. It seems to me that one can only justify painful experimentation if one can find clear rational grounds for saying that human interests are always and absolutely primary. Accepting that it may be sometimes right to choose in the interests of humans is one thing; believing that we are justified in creating an institution that routinely uses and abuses animals is another. But I also accept that others judge the matter differently, and that honourable people may honourably disagree.

IV

Despite my viewpoint, I have been reluctant to comment on the latest round of controversy at Oxford. The reason is that I have not wanted to appear to give succour or support to those who pursue violent tactics or intimidation. Some have been surprised that I wouldn't join the protests, but they shouldn't be. If I cannot accept the utilitarian argument of researchers that the end justifies the means, by the same standard, I cannot accept the utilitarian argument of violent protestors that their intended ends justify their means.

It is especially lamentable that people who are committed to a philosophy of respect for all sentient beings (as I am myself) should think that violence, coercion, and personal abuse is justifiable against human sentient beings. Violence is not just counterproductive or bad tactics; it is morally self-contradictory. One cannot get to animal rights by trampling on human ones. As someone who has experienced abuse and defamation for my work for animals, and lost job opportunities as a result of my views on animal testing, I think I have earned the right to say that personal attacks are as unconscionable as they are (almost always) ineffective.

Neither do I support illegality; however dotty or unjust laws may be, we are obligated to obey them, at least in a democratic society, where we have the ability to change the laws. In a democracy, criminal tactics are an attempt to shortcut the system. As I wrote way back in 1994: "To pursue moral means requires that we reject strategies of blatant manipulation and intimidation. Not to do so risks not a decrease but an increase in the total amount of moral evil in the world today … People will not be easily cajoled, intimidated, threatened or bludgeoned beyond their moral senses into a new world; they need to be rationally persuaded".[23]

V

I conclude with a very modest proposal: rational dialogue. What we need is dialogue without personal or political agendas. If such dialogue cannot take place within universities, where else can it be had? Certainly not in the media, who frequently succumb to sensationalist and frankly inaccurate reporting. A great university – as Oxford undoubtedly is – could lead the way in fostering and facilitating such dialogue. In doing so, it would accept the integrity of differing viewpoints, and give power to the conviction that reasoning can be one way of apprehending the fullness of moral truth.

The animal issue is not going to go away. Over the last 40 years, we have slowly but surely experienced a paradigm shift: a move away from the old idea that animals are just things, machines, tools, commodities, resources here for us to the idea that animals have intrinsic value, dignity, and rights. It is simply no longer clear to many people that human interests are the only important interests in the world, and that all other interests – including those of animals – should always be subordinate to ours. Oxford may be wary of this new paradigm, even uneasy with its own anti-vivisection history, but my hope is that it may yet find an appropriate and positive response to the growing ethical sensitivity to animals – a sensitivity which it has, in part, helped to inspire and pioneer.

Notes

1   John Ruskin, letter in *Pall Mall Gazette*, Vol. XXXiii, p. 1vi. See John Bowker, "Religions and the Rights of Animals" (introduction) in Tom Regan (ed), *Animal Sacrifices: Religious Perspectives on the Use of Animals in Science* (Philadelphia: Temple University Press, 1986), p. 3. A flavour of the debate is captured in a cartoon of 1883, titled "A Collection for Vivisection", where vivisection is "equated with the trials of an undergraduate at a termly examination", Paul Weindling, "The University's

Contribution to the Life Sciences and Medicine" in John Prest (ed), *The Illustrated History of Oxford University* (Oxford: Oxford University Press, 1993), p. 282.

2   Lewis Carroll (Charles L. Dodgson), *Some Popular Fallacies about Vivisection*, printed for private circulation, Oxford, June 1875.

3   See Lori Williamson, *Power and Protest: Frances Power Cobbe and Victorian Society* (London: Rivers Oram Press, 2005), pp. 125f. Cobbe had a long-time friendship with the then Principal of Manchester College, James Martineau, who supported her work. There is a plaque in the College commemorating Cobbe's achievements.

4   E. B. Nicholson, *The Rights of an Animal: A New Essay in Ethics* (London: C. Kegan Paul, 1879).

5   Peter Singer, *Animal Liberation: A New Ethics for Our Treatment of Animals* (London: Jonathan Cape, 1976).

6   Stephen R. L. Clark, *The Moral Status of Animals* (Oxford: The Clarendon Press, 1977).

7   Stanley and Roslind Godlovitch and John Harris (eds) *Animals, Men and Morals: An Inquiry into the Maltreatment of Non-Humans* (London: Victor Gollancz, 1971).

8   See his review of *Animals, Men and Morals* in the *New York Review of Books*, 5 April, 1973.

9   Andrew Linzey, *Animal Rights: A Christian Assessment* (London: SCM Press, 1976).

10 For an excellent summary of the empirical evidence, see David DeGrazia, *Taking Animals Seriously: Mental Life and Moral Status* (Cambridge: Cambridge University Press, 1996), especially chapter 7.

11 C. S. Lewis, *The Problem of Pain* (London: Geoffrey Bles, 1940), p. 117.

12 I am grateful to Professor Dan Robinson of Georgetown University for this term.

13 I develop the case at length in Andrew Linzey, *Why Animal Suffering Matters*, forthcoming.

14 See Andrew Linzey, *Animal Theology* (London: SCM Press and Chicago: University of Illinois Press, 1994), see pp. 56f.

15 For a variety of views, see "Souls and Redemption" in Andrew Linzey and Dorothy Yamamoto (eds), *Animals on the Agenda: Questions about Animals for Theology and Ethics* (London: SCM Press, and Chicago: University of

16 C. S. Lewis, "Vivisection", first published as a booklet by the New England Anti-Vivisection Society [1947] and in Walter Hooper (ed) *Undeceptions: Essays on Theology and Ethics* (London: Geoffrey Bles, 1952), pp. 182-6, also reprinted in Andrew Linzey and Tom Regan (eds), *Animals and Christianity: A Book of Readings* (London: SCM Press, and New York: Crossroad, 1989; reprinted by Wipf and Stock, 2008), pp. 160-4. People often ask how this publication came about. The answer is that the then Vice-Chancellor of Oxford, Sir Richard W. Livingstone, drew the attention of his friend, George N. Farnum, to Lewis' concern about animal suffering exemplified in his book *The Problem of Pain*. Farnum was President of the New England Anti-Vivisection Society and immediately wrote to Lewis asking if he would write for the cause. Farnum explains the genesis of the paper in his foreword to the original 1947 pamphlet.

17 Terry Waite, *Taken on Trust* (London: Hodder and Stoughton, 1993), p. xiii.

18 Andrew Linzey, *Animal Theology*, p. 33.

19 R. G. Frey, *Rights, Killing and Suffering: Moral Vegetarianism and Applied Ethics* (Oxford: Blackwell, 1983), p. 115.

20 The key text here is Susan E. Lederer, *Subjected to Science: Human Experimentation in America before the Second World War* (Baltimore: The Johns Hopkins University Press, 1995). It is clear from the book that Lederer is not herself an anti-vivisectionist, indeed she is not wholly unfavourable to both experimentation on human as well as animal subjects. All the more remarkable, then, that one of her documented claims is that "During this period [before the Second World War], the moral issues raised by experimenting on human beings were most intensely pursued by men and women committed to the protection of animals. Already devoted to saving dogs, cats and other animals from the vivisector's knife, anti-vivisectionists warned that the replacement of the family physician by the 'scientists by the bedside' would inspire non-therapeutic experimentation on vulnerable human beings". Again: "Human vivisection must be understood in the larger context of animal protection", pp. xiv and xv. Taken from Andrew Linzey, *Animal Gospel* (London: Hodder and Stoughton, and Louisville, Kentucky: Westminster John Knox Press, 1999), pp. 92-8.

21 See Paul A. B. Clarke and Andrew Linzey, *Research on Embryos: Politics, Theology and Law* (London: LCAP, 1988).

22 *Your Baby and Your Dog* (New York: Vivisection Investigation League, nd), cited in Lederer, *Subjected to Science*, p. 101; original emphases.
23 Andrew Linzey, *Animal Gospel*, chapter 10, pp. 90-1. The chapter is an expanded version of an article that first appeared in the *Times Higher Educational Supplement*, 23 December, 1994.

This article is a revised version of the University Sermon preached at the University Church, Oxford, on 17 February, 2008. The author would like to thank Canon Vincent Strudwick and Professor Priscilla Cohn for their comments on an earlier draft.

בס"ד

Pope Benedict and the Jews
James R. Michaels

The death of Pope John Paul II in 2005, and the election of Cardinal Joseph Ratzinger to the papacy, was met by expressions of concern in the organized Jewish community, as well as among individual Jews around the world. Pope John Paul II was universally acknowledged to have done much to improve relations between the Catholic Church and the Jewish people. Among his many acts of reconciliation, one could count the things which were symbolic—a visit to Auschwitz in 1979, his frequent contacts with the chief rabbi of Rome, and his visit to a synagogue in Rome–and substantive, such as his revision of the official Church teaching which contained a historic change in the depiction of Jews. At the time of its publication, experts such as Eugene Fisher pointed out that this change would bring a new message of conciliation around the world, including places where few or no Jews exist.[1]

In the days following Cardinal Ratzinger's election as pope, stories were published relating that he had been a member of the Hitler Youth during his adolescent years. Many Jews harbor suspicions about Germans who lived during the Nazi era, and this revelation added to their concern that Pope Benedict might reverse many of the achievements of his predecessor. His official position in the Vatican had been director of the Congregation for the Doctrine of the Faith, once officially known as the Holy Office of the Inquisition. The memory of the experience of Jews during the Inquisition in Spain, Italy, and even Mexico still resonates with many Jews; this fact about Cardinal Ratzinger's past stoked concerns, although there was no evidence that he had ever used his office to the detriment of Jews.[2]

Shortly after his election, Pope Benedict made some symbolic gestures which helped to allay the concerns of Jews. He paid a visit to Germany and visited a synagogue which had been restored after the Holocaust. He also visited Auschwitz in 2006. While there, he said, "The rulers of the Third Reich wanted to crush the entire Jewish people, to cancel it from the register of the peoples of the earth. Deep down, those vicious criminals, by wiping out this people, wanted to kill the God who laid down principles to serve as a guide for mankind, principles that are entirely valid." [3]

I. Summorum Pontificum

These gestures were well received in the Jewish community, but fears were raised once again in July 2007 with the release of the pope's apostolic letter *Summorum Pontificum*, on the use of the Roman liturgy prior to the reform of 1970. The decree eased restrictions on the use of the 1962 Roman Missal, the Latin (Tridentine) Mass which was standard before the new Order of the Mass was introduced in 1970.

Of specific concern was the Good Friday liturgy in the 1962 Roman rite which contains a call for the conversion of Jews who are considered "blind" and for God to lift the "veil from their hearts" so that they might know Jesus Christ. In the 1970 reform of the liturgy inspired by the Second Vatican Council these prayers were modified to affirm the biblical covenant between God and the Jewish people.[4]

Summorum Pontificum was issued as a *motu proprio* (lit. "of his own accord"), which is officially defined as a personal papal executive order, the provisions of which are decided by the pope for reasons which he himself deems sufficient.[5] As such, it could be interpreted as reflecting the will of the pope, and possibly signaling a change of policy regarding the wording in the Latin Mass which Jews found offensive.

Jewish leaders involved in ongoing dialogue with the Catholic Church were quick to express their concern. The most strident was Abraham Foxman of the Anti Defamation League who, even before the pope's decision had been made public, issued a statement calling it a "body blow to Catholic-Jewish relations." Others were more muted in their comments, but focused on the specific question of whether the pope intended to permit churches on Good Friday to recite the prayer which called for the conversion of the "perfidious Jews."[6]

Allowing the prayer to be read, Jewish communal officials said, would appear to run counter to the spirit of *Nostra Aetate*, the landmark 1965 Vatican declaration, and subsequent reforms that absolved Jews of responsibility for the killing of Jesus and laid the groundwork for four decades of improved Catholic-Jewish relations. In particular, Jewish groups said that a prayer to convert the Jews would undermine previous steps taken by the church recognizing the validity of Judaism.[7] The two chief rabbis of Israel also jointly wrote a letter to the pope asking for clarification.[8]

The Vatican appeared surprised and unprepared to respond to the reaction. A few days later, in a letter to bishops, the pope wrote, "There is no contradiction between the two editions of the Roman Missal. In the history of the liturgy there is growth and progress, but no rupture. What earlier generations held as sacred remains sacred and great for us, too, and it cannot be all of a sudden entirely forbidden or even considered harmful. It behooves all of us to preserve the riches which have developed in the church's faith and prayer and to give them their proper place."[9]

Vatican officials also pointed out that this was not a new issue, and that in July 1988 Pope John Paul II had issued his own *motu proprio*, *Ecclesia Dei*, in which he had granted a limited use of the Tridentine liturgy. He wrote, "respect must everywhere be shown for the feelings of all those who are attached to the Latin liturgical tradition."[10]

In response, the American Jewish Committee expressed its appreciation for the explanation. "We acknowledge that the Church's liturgy is an internal Catholic matter and this *motu proprio* from Pope Benedict XVI is based on the permission given by John Paul II in 1988 and thus, on principle, is nothing new," said Rabbi David Rosen, AJC's international director of Interreligious Affairs. "However we are naturally concerned about how wider use of this Tridentine liturgy may impact upon how Jews are perceived and treated."[11]

Rosen added, "Contrary to those who presented the *motu proprio* as a retreat from advances in Catholic-Jewish relations, this clarification in effect confirms those strides and even advances them."[12] Later in July, Cardinal Tarcisio Bertone, Vatican secretary of state, told reporters that the problem of the Good Friday prayer would be studied at the Vatican and might be resolved by deciding that even those who use the 1962 missal would use the 1970 text of the prayer. A spokesman for the Israeli chief rabbis said members of the Jewish community expect the Vatican to fulfill promises to correct the situation.[13]

In the months that followed the issue of the pope's *motu proprio*, much was done to put the issue in context. Catholic leaders said that, in essence, it was a pastoral issue, not theological or polemical, and designed to foster reconciliation within the Church. Rev. Thomas Rosica wrote the pope's decision was motivated "by a desire to bring about 'an interior reconciliation in the heart of the church.' Benedict simply wishes to support reconciliation among Catholics and to reconcile the church with its liturgical past."[14] A Catholic journal wrote, "Pope Benedict insists he is not taking the church on a nostalgia trip. He wants to re-energize it, and hopes that the Latin Mass, like an immense celestial object, will exert gravitational pull on the faithful."[15] Another journal wrote, "Part of the purpose of the letter, as Benedict says, is to ease the way toward reconciliation with the Lefebvrists of the Society of St. Pius X. He recognizes that their schism involves deeper theological questions, including the recognition of the authority of the Second Vatican Council, but this is one step toward healing the wound of schism."[16]

Experience in a small community in Northeast Pennsylvania demonstrates the sensitivities of Jews to the wording of the Tridentine Mass. For many years, a sign near the Grotto of Our Lady of Fatima in Wilkes-Barre, PA in the Diocese of Scranton, proclaimed that the Tridentine Mass would be offered each week in a local church "with the authority of Pope John Paul II." Although the sign was small, it attracted the attention of Jews who were concerned that some Catholics were attempting on a local level to undo the gains achieved by *Nostra Aetate*.[17]

Rev. Philip Altavilla, director of the Office of Ecumenism and Interfaith Affairs for the Diocese of Scranton and a native of Wilkes-Barre, explained that the group which placed the sign probably picked up on the permission granted by Pope John Paul II in his *motu proprio,* and didn't support anything that was contrary to his wishes. Indeed, he said, the Priestly Fraternity of Saint Peter, a group loyal to the Holy Father and in communion with him, regularly offers the Tridentine liturgy. They are a group of former Lefebvrists who, in 1988, sought and were granted reconciliation with the Catholic Church.[18]

Catholics in the Diocese of Scranton have had a long history of cooperation with their Jewish neighbors. Addressing this issue, Rev. Altavilla said Catholic laity wouldn't require that the old way of referring to the Jews remain in the Latin Liturgy. "I think they would understand the importance of using the 1970 translation." He added, "I would say that with the atmosphere of positive relations that has developed between Roman Catholics and the Jewish community, a majority of people would not miss anything negative that would have been removed, for good reason."

In January 2008, it was announced that Pope Benedict had decided to modify "completely" the controversial prayer for the conversion of Jews in the Good Friday liturgy. *Il Giornale* newspaper said this would involve at least the removal of a reference to Jewish "blindness" but the changes could be more extensive. It was expected that the new text would be announced before Good Friday, 2008.[19]

Why did Pope Benedict issue his *motu proprio* when he did? And why was the Vatican unprepared and surprised at the reaction from Jews? Rev. Philip Altavilla said that it was aimed at bringing reconciliation with the Lefebvrists, and that no consideration had been paid to how Jews might react. Dr. Eugene Fisher, former Associate Director of the Secretariat for Ecumenical and Interreligious Affairs of the United States Conference of Catholic Bishops, suggested that *Summorum Pontificum* was issued without consulting about the possible impact and implications. "People in authority should have talked with each other but didn't," he said. "It has happened before." Dr. Fisher also thinks that the new pope isn't accustomed to the scrutiny paid to what he says. In the past, he would cite obscure texts and statements, but nobody would comment. Now every news outlet in the world pays attention. (This may account for comments and statements which have angered representatives of other faith groups.)

Rabbi Mark Shook, of St. Louis, MO, who has been involved in Jewish-Catholic dialogue for many years, thinks that the use of the Latin Mass will be used to revive struggling churches. In St. Louis, the Bishop assigned declining churches in ethnic communities to use the Latin Mass. He also doubts that the *motu proprio* was intended to derail the spirit of cooperation between Jews and Catholics. "As someone who has seen the resurgence of Hebrew as a unifying factor all over the world, I think there is a tremendous value in having a language of the faith. But when you have gone to the trouble, after 2,000 years, of transforming the relationship between the church and non-Catholic religions, why would you want to take a leap backward?"[20]

The permission to return to the Latin Mass has met with more popularity than originally expected. For example, in the Diocese of Arlington VA, several churches are instituting the rite; mostly younger people, who have no memory of when the Mass was recited exclusively in Latin, are attending. A priest in Chicago has also started a web site offering instruction in the ritual.[21]

It is beyond the scope of this article to examine the extent of the response to *Summorum Pontificum* throughout North America or, indeed, the world. Further research would be fruitful to chart the popularity of the revival of the Tridentine mass, and whether its return carries any implication of dissatisfaction for other changes brought about by and after Vatican II.

II. Pope Benedict's past, and its implications for the future.

The issue of *Summorum Pontificum* aside, it is fruitful to examine the past of Pope Benedict, and to see if there are any indications of the direction he will take the Church in the area of Jewish-Catholic relations. As noted above, he was a young boy when Hitler came to power. His father was anti-Nazi, but young Joseph Ratzinger was required to join Hitler Youth. Although attendance at meetings was required for him to get a substantial reduction of tuition at seminary, he finessed the matter and skipped most meetings. Later, he was drafted into the army, but did not fight because of a physical illness. After the war he was briefly imprisoned as a POW, but released after a few months. He then returned to his seminary studies. Representatives of Yad Va'Shem, the Holocaust Memorial in Jerusalem, and the Simon Wiesenthal Center in Los Angeles have both said that further investigation into his involvement in Nazi activities is not warranted.[22]

Carindal Ratzinger was known to represent the more conservative element in the Church. This apparently stemmed from experiences when he was teaching in the 1960's and was treated rudely by secularists in his classes. Apparently, he combines his strong conservatism with a favorable view of Judaism and Jews as facing the same threats as Catholics from liberalism and secularism. When he was in position to do something about it, he did. According to Rev. Rosica, Cardinal Ratzinger wrote all of John Paul II's statements on the Jews. "He personally prepared *Memory and Reconciliation*, the 2000 document outlining the church's historical 'errors' in its treatment of Jews. And as president of the Pontifical Biblical Commission, Ratzinger oversaw the preparation of *The Jewish People and Their Sacred Scriptures in the Christian Bible*, a milestone theological explanation for the Jews' rejection of Jesus."[23]

Cardinal Ratzinger also made known his own views before he was elected Pope. For example, he wrote, "Jews and Christians should accept each other in profound inner reconciliation, neither in disregard of their faith nor in its denial, but out of the depth of faith itself. In their mutual reconciliation they should become a force for peace in and for the world.[24]

Just before Christmas in 2000, he wrote, "Our gratitude, therefore, must be extended to our Jewish brothers and sisters who, despite the hardships of their own history, have held on to faith in this God right up to the present...Perhaps it is precisely because of this latest tragedy that a new vision of the relationship between the Church and Israel has been born: a sincere willingness to overcome every kind of anti-Judaism, and to initiate a constructive dialogue based on knowledge of each other, and on reconciliation."[25]

In one of his first acts after his election, Pope Benedict noted the 40th anniversary of *Nostra Aetate*. He said it "gives us abundant reason to express gratitude to Almighty God for the witness of all those who, despite a complex and often painful history, and especially after the tragic experience of the Shoah, which was inspired by a neo-pagan racist ideology, worked courageously to foster reconciliation and improved understanding between Christians and Jews."

Benedict expressed hope that Christians and Jews will offer

"shared witness to the One God and His commandments, the sanctity of life, the promotion of human dignity, the rights of the family and the need to build a world of justice, reconciliation and peace for future generations."[26] Rabbi David Rosen of the American Jewish Committee believes the pope is committed to continuing strong ties to Jews.[27]

In the fall of 2007, Pope Benedict set forth his personal theology in his book *Jesus of Nazareth* (Doubleday). The preface, signed "Joseph Ratzinger, Pope Benedict XVI," states, "This work is not an absolute act of magisterial teaching, but merely an expression of my personal research into the face of the Lord."[28] As such, it is indicative of the direction he will give to the Church.

Although primarily a review of the Christian Scriptures as a way of explaining his belief of who and what Jesus was, the pope also pays some attention to the Jewish view of Jesus, both while he lived and thereafter. He enlists the help of Rabbi Jacob Neusner, a prominent Jewish scholar and historian. Neusner has also written books for popular consumption, including *A Rabbi Talks with Jesus* (Doubleday, 1993). He wrote his book with the intention to "renew the centuries-old tradition of disputation between Catholics and Jews."[29] Before publication, the book was sent to Cardinal Ratzinger for comment and recommendation. In his own book, Pope Benedict XVI uses the questions asked by Neusner to help demonstrate his admiration for Jews and Judaism. He writes, "Let us try to draw out the essential points of [Neusner's theoretical] conversation in order to know Jesus and to understand our Jewish brothers better."[30]

The Pope notes Neusner's concern about the call of Jesus to follow him, instead of the Torah. He writes that Neusner "rightly sees this commandment as anchoring the heart of the social order.... It is this family of Israel that is threatened by Jesus' message, and the foundations of Israel's social order are thrust aside by the primacy of his person."[31] "Neusner thus concludes: 'I now realize, only God can demand of me what Jesus is asking.' "[32]

Benedict responds: "All in all, it would be good for the Christian world to look respectfully at this obedience of Israel, and thus to appreciate better the great commandments of the Decalogue, which Christians have to transfer into the context of God's universal family and which Jesus, as the 'new Moses,' has given to us."[33]

The pope writes that Jewish reluctance to accept Jesus as Messiah is based on a well reasoned and deeply felt desire to maintain what is central to Judaism: belief in one God, maintaining the social order of Israel, and caring for the rights of all. Christians should allow Jews' adherence to these principles to goad them into greater service of others. "It is our Jewish interlocutors who, quite rightly, ask again and again, so what has your 'Messiah' Jesus actually brought? He has not brought world peace, and he has not conquered the world's misery. So he can hardly be the true Messiah."[34] This is connected with a further point: The fundamental norm in the Torah, on which everything depends, is insistence upon faith in the one God (YHWH): He alone may be worshiped. But now, as the Prophets develop the Torah, responsibility for the poor, widows, and orphans gradually ascends to the same level as the exclusive worship of the one God.[35]

It can be deduced, therefore, that Pope Benedict's image of Jews coincides with his own view of what the Church should be: a force for maintaining the social order, insuring the rights of all (presumably including the unborn), and a bulwark against secularism. Although this may be an oversimplification of what Jews believe, it certainly indicates that he will continue to encourage dialogue and cooperation between Jews and Catholics. Catholics who know Pope Benedict XVI, and are familiar with his thought and writings, are confident that he will do so.[36]

III. The future of Jewish-Catholic cooperation

The question could also be asked if the Church as an institution will continue this dialogue and cooperation after Pope Benedict has exited the scene. This should be of concern, given the pope's age, the historical tendency of the Church to follow a long-serving pope with one who serves only a few years, and the possibility that sometime in the future a candidate from the Third World will be elected pope.

Again, the answer is a resounding Yes! Due to the work of Jewish and Catholic leaders for over 40 years, and the progress made in that time, several facts are firmly in place within the Church. Rabbi Gilbert Rosenthal points out that in the years after the publication of *Nostra Aetate*, several documents fleshed out the principles it established. These include official guidelines for presenting Jews and Judaism in sermons and teaching, as well as a reflection on the Shoah. These documents form part of the *Magisterium* – the body of teachings of the Catholic Church.[37] To try to unravel what has taken place through two major Pontificates would be virtually impossible.[38]

The Vatican's own web site prominently displays *The Jewish People and their Sacred Scriptures in the Bible*, affirming the validity of the Jewish covenant established with Abraham. Written by the Pontifical Biblical Commission in 2001, the paper was overseen and praised by then Cardinal Joseph Ratzinger.[39]

Theologically, Church leaders have and are still grappling with the realization that persistent Jewish teachings against Jews had made the Holocaust possible. Church leaders continue to work to eliminate these teachings from official Church policy and the minds of Roman Catholics.[40] This has resulted in two major changes in church policy:

- The charge of deicide has been removed completely from Catholic textbooks.
- The Catholic Church allocates no resources for the conversion of the Jews.[41]

One notable result of this continuing cooperation was seen in the immediate aftermath of *Summorum Pontificum*. The Vatican issued a statement from the Commission for the Religious Relations with the Jews affirming that there was "no intention whatsoever to change the contents of the teachings of *Nostra Aetate* concerning the relations between the Church and the Jewish People."[42]

Conclusions

Despite early concerns by Jews, and unfortunate logistical mistakes by the pope and those who advise him, it can be concluded that Pope Benedict XVI personally believes that dialogue and cooperation between Catholics and Jews should continue. Moreover, even if he did not hold this personal commitment, the apparatus of the Church would preserve the achievements made after *Nostra Aetate*. Even during the brief controversy created by Pope Benedict's *motu proprio*, the trend continued: Throughout the second half of 2007, clergy and laity from various dioceses traveled to Israel and Auschwitz, and dialogue continued in many communities. Rev. Philip Altavilla in the Diocese of Scranton stated it simply, "All meetings and dialogues are continuing. We're still making steady progress."

Post Script

On February 5, 2008, the Vatican announced the new wording for the Latin liturgy for Good Friday. The new prayer deletes the reference to Jews' "blindness", as well as the call that God "may lift the veil from their hearts." However, it includes language that reads, "Let us pray for the Jews. May the Lord Our God enlighten their hearts so that they may acknowledge Jesus Christ, the savior of all men." This was again greeted by statements of protest and dismay from various Jewish groups. Rabbi David Rosen from the American Jewish Committee said, "Pope Benedict XVI really does care about positive Catholic-Jewish relations — that I know for a fact. It is therefore particularly disappointing that this text doesn't seem to show any sensitivity as to how this new text will be read within Jewish circles."⁴³

The following day, Auxiliary Bishop Richard Sklba of Milwaukee, on behalf of the United States Conference of Bishops, issued a statement which reaffirmed the U.S. Church's commitment to "deepening its bonds of friendship and mutual understanding with the Jewish community."⁴⁴ Eugene Fisher said that the wording is eschatological in nature, and not intended to signal a new policy of the Church to convert Jews to Catholicism. He acknowledged, however, that the prayer is ambiguous and confusing, and therefore requires more dialogue and a clarification from Rome about the new prayer's intent.

In the course of researching this article, I gained an appreciation of Pope Benedict's desire to promote and continue Jewish-Catholic dialogue and cooperation. If members of the hierarchy of the Church truly wish to build and strengthen bridges between the two communities, however, I believe they should be more aware of Jewish sensitivities. Twice within one year, the Church has issued statements which are potentially offensive to Jews, then relied on others to clarify them. This trend will not advance the cause all parties agree is important and necessary.

The following specialists in Jewish-Christian relations were consulted while researching this paper:

Rev. Philip A. Altavilla V.E. is Episcopal Vicar, Northern Pastoral Region and Director of the Office of Ecumenism and Interfaith Affairs, Diocese of Scranton.

Dr. Eugene J. Fisher served as Associate Director of the Secretariat for Ecumenical and Interreligious Affairs of the United States Conference of Catholic Bishops from 1977 until 2007. He is a

Consultor to the Holy See's Commission for Religious Relations with the Jews.

Rabbi Gilbert Rosenthal is the former executive vice president of the New York Board of Rabbis and director of the National Council of Synagogues. He co-produced six films, *Walking God's Paths: Christians and Jews in Candid Conversation*. His most recent book is *What Can a Modern Jew Believe?* (Wipf and Stock)

Father Thomas Rosica is CEO of the Salt and Light Catholic Television Network in Canada. From 1994-2006 he served as the Canadian Bishops' Representative on the National Christian-Jewish Consultation.

Rabbi Mark Shook is Interfaith Chair of the St. Louis Rabbinical Association, which conducts an ongoing dialogue with priests from the Archdiocese of St. Louis.

Notes

1 Throughout this article, reference will be made to conversations and email communications with various experts in the field of Catholic-Jewish relations. Their official titles and credentials are listed at the end of the text.
2 *Profile: Pope Benedict XVI*, www.BBC.CO.UK, September 15, 2006.
3 *Pope Benedict's Auschwitz Prayer*, Time Magazine, May. 29, 2006
4 Sacred Heart University, Center for Christian-Jewish Understanding, July 18, 2007
5 *New Advent, Catholic Encyclopedia*. www.newadvent.org.
6 Vatican move on Latin Mass sparks outrage from Jews, *Jewish Telegraphic Agency*, July 10, 2007.
7 Ibid
8 The two major Jewish communities of Israel–Ashkenazim (Jews

of European descent) and Sephardim (descendants of Jews from Mediterranean lands)–each have a chief rabbi.

9 Letter to Bishops, July 7, 2007
10 The complete text of this document can be found on the Vatican Website, www.vatican.va
11 American Jewish Committee, press release, July 9, 2007
12 American Jewish Committee, press release, July 19, 2007
13 Catholic-Jewish Relations: Bumps in the road should not slow the journey, Catholic News Service, August, 17, 2007
14 Rosica, *Toronto Sun*, August 12, 2007
15 The Pope Reopens a Portal to Eternity, via the 1950s, *Editorial Observer*, July 29, 2007
16 The Pope's Liturgical Liberalism, *First Things, The Journal of Religion, Culture and Public Life*, July 9, 2007.
17 The author of this article resided in Wilkes-Barre from 1988 until 1998. He often heard questions and conversations among Jews about the sign.
18 A representative of the Fraternity said, following the innovation of Pope John XXIII in 1962, they had always omitted the word "perfidious" from the Good Friday liturgy. He said they understand that they are praying for Jews, and "we hope the Jews pray for us."
19 Catholic News Service, January 18, 2008.
20 *Resurrecting the Rite*, St. Louis Magazine, October, 2007
21 *Latin Mass Makes a Comeback*, Washington Post, November 24, 2007
22 *New Pope Defied Nazis as Teen*, New York Times, April 23, 2005
23 *Ratzinger a Nazi? Don't believe it*, The Jerusalem Post, April 18, 2005
24 Ratzinger, Joseph Cardinal, *Reconciling Gospel and Torah: the Catechism*
25 Ratzinger, Joseph Cardinal, *The Heritage of Abraham: The Gift of Christmas*. L'Osservatore Romano - 29 December 2000
26 A bond between great religions, Toronto Sun, November 6, 2005
27 Time Magazine, May, 29, 2006
28 Ratzinger, Joseph, Pope Benedict XVI, *Jesus of Nazareth*, 2007, xxiv
29 Renewing Religious Disputation in Quest of Theological Truth, *Communio*, Summer 2007, p. 334
30 *Jesus of Nazereth*, 104

31 Ibid. 113
32 Ibid. 115
33 Ibid. 122
34 Ibid. 116
35 Ibid. 125
36 "Symposium: Christian-Jewish Relations, Nostra Aetate at Forty," *Midstream,* September/October 2005. P. 12
37 Ibid. p. 18
38 *Midstream* symposium, P. 12
39 *The Jewish People and their Sacred Scriptures in the Bible,* www.vatican.va.
40 Ibid
41 Ibid, p 13
42 Boston College, Center for Christian-Jewish Learning, July 23, 2007
43 New York Times, February 6, 2008
44 Zenit.org, February 7, 2008

Religion Without God: Exploring the Perimeters of Huxley's Humanism*

John H. Morgan

Before exploring the scientific humanism of Sir Julian Huxley as a substitute for a supernatural religion, I thought it might be helpful to establish sound footing with respect to the definition of "religion" as used in the social and behavioral sciences. As Huxley was so very insistent upon the central role of the human community in the directing of the continuing evolutionary saga of the universe, to look to the study of society and culture through the investigative mechanisms of the behavioral and social sciences seems, therefore, quite fitting. Huxley, trained in the biological sciences, was quite keen to point to and draw from those working in the social sciences as relates to the human condition, and no one in the early twenty-first century can be thought of more highly in this regard than is Professor Clifford Geertz of the Institute for Advanced Studies at Princeton, formerly Distinguished Eastman Professor at Oxford University, Huxley's own *alma mater* and teaching venue. Once we have established the basis and perimeters of the concept of "religion" as employed by social scientists, we will revisit Huxley's notion of scientific (often called "evolutionary") humanism to see if and where there might be a convergence of understanding.

In an attempt to blaze a humanistic path between positivism

and functionalism, Geertz has put forth what is increasingly being considered the most useful definition of religion to date in the social sciences. "The view of man as a symbolizing, conceptualizing, meaning-seeking animal," Geertz has pointed out in his essay, entitled, "Ethos, World-View and the Analysis of Sacred Symbols," in the *Antioch Review*, "opens a whole new approach to the analysis of religion." While attempting to demonstrate the legitimate perimeters of the social sciences, and especially anthropology, in analyzing religious phenomena, Geertz conscientiously withholds any challenge to the methodological credibility of the history and phenomenology of religions in the pursuit of the "essence of religious experience." This "essence" Geertz, like all self-respecting social scientists, will wisely steer clear of while focusing, rather, upon the behavioral aspects of religious practice.

The following definition has been acclaimed throughout the social scientific community as a most comprehensive endeavor to do justice to behavior without doing violence to the ideology behind behavior. Let us take a closer look. This definition first appeared in an essay by Geertz in 1966 entitled, "Religion as a Cultural System," in an anthology edited by M. Banton under the title, *Anthropological Approaches to the Study of Religion*, though it has now been reprinted in countless other places since it has moved into the public domain as a standard stock-in-trade operating definition by social scientists. "Religion," says Geertz, "is (1) a system of symbols which acts to (2) establish powerful, persuasive, and long lasting moods and motivations in men by (3) formulating conceptions of a general order of existence and (4) clothing these conceptions with such an aura of factuality that (5) the moods and motivations seem uniquely realistic."

The design, obviously, is not to construct a definitive definition which exhausts all dimensions of religious phenomena, but rather to construct a realistic and useable definition with intentional limitations and specificity of scope. Concurring with, but not limiting himself to, Yinger's definition of religion as a "system of beliefs and practices by means of which a group of people struggles with ultimate problems of human life" (J. Milton Yinger, *The Scientific Study of Religion*, NY: Macmillan, 1970), Geertz suggests that a fundamental characteristic of religion is the address to the "problem of meaning" meaning suggesting purpose and direction to life and meaninglessness suggesting chaos and pointless existence. "There are at least three points," says Geertz, "where chaos — a tumult of events which lack not just interpretation but interpretability — threatens to break in upon man at the limits of his analytic capacities, at the limits of his powers of endurance, and at the limits of his moral insight. *Bafflement, suffering, and a sense of intractable ethical paradox* are all radical challenges with which any religion, however 'primitive,' which hopes to persist must attempt somehow to cope." Here, of course, we will eventually bring humanism to bear upon this functional definition of religion as a mechanism to respond to the inexorability of life's experiences and challenges.

Without doing an injustice to the social scientific perspective of Geertz, we can say that religion constitutes an experientially motivated address to the problem of impending chaos in the existential experience of human existence. Furthermore, we can say that beyond, behind, or under religion's capacity to cope with bafflement, suffering, and inextricable ethical paradox lies the *essence of meaning* to which these expressions are enduring witnesses. This implied extension cannot, of course, be pursued in this essay, but I have considered it elsewhere ("Religion and Culture as Meaning Systems," in the 1977 October issue of *The Journal of Religion*). Geertz, of course, is not oblivious to this possible extension and logical elaboration of his position, nor is he antipathetic to such an endeavor. "The problem of meaning in each of its integrating aspects," he continues, "is a matter of affirming, or at least recognizing, the inescapability of *ignorance, pain, and injustice* on the human plane while simultaneously denying that these irrationalities are characteristic of the world as a whole."

Even an elementary acquaintance with the history of the scientific study of religion is sufficient to establish the qualitative advance Geertz's definition has made, especially as he employs the concept of meaning as an interpretive tool. Within his definitional construct, Geertz stands head and shoulders above recent efforts to understand religion by the positivists and functionalists. If Huxley and the humanists have produced a religion without God, then here might just be the starting place for our investigation.

"The existence of bafflement, pain and moral paradox — of the Problem of Meaning," says Geertz, "is one of the things that drive men toward belief in gods, devils, spirits, totemic principles, or the spiritual efficacy of cannibalism, but it is not the basis upon which those beliefs rest, but rather their most important field of application." Here is the beginning point for scientific humanism, namely, to recognize that religious expression grows out of religious experience, and it is precisely this "experience" which Huxley and the humanists choose to identify as possible even in the absence of a supernatural infrastructure. This "drive toward belief" is conveyed through cultural symbols and bespeaks the human quest for meaning, for an existential meaning, that is, challenges chaos and which pursues order. "Whatever else religion may be," Geertz says, and the humanists must listen carefully here, "it is in part an attempt (of an implicit and directly felt rather than explicit and consciously thought-about sort) to conserve the fund of general meanings in terms of which each individual interprets his experience and organizes his conduct."

Huxley's scientific humanism must be informed by the social scientific understanding of the meaning and nature of religious expression as it relates to cultural expression. Culture and religion, after all, are both symbol-systems which express humankind's quest for meaning. *If humanism can step into this caldron and offer an experientially self-validating sense of meaning and purpose without the benefit of an intervening power source external to the phenomenal world, then humanism has a chance at embodying the fundamental ingredients of religion*. Any serious convergence of cultural and religious expressions necessarily centers around the experience of meaning, an experience which is multi-dimensional and expressed through symbols. Though culture is historically transmitted as patterns of meaning which are embodied in a complex of symbols, Geertz contends that "meanings can only be 'stored' in symbols," and are not synonymous with the symbols themselves. Positivists attempt to equate "meanings" with "symbols" themselves, whilst functionalists attempt to equate the social "functions" of meaning-symbols with meanings themselves. Whereas culture and religion are convergent expressions of meaning, anthropology and theology (systematic expressions of religiously motivated ideological constructs) are disciplines addressed to the systematics of meaning, and as noted above, the analysis of meaning will inevitably involve an analysis of the symbol as meaning-bearer.

Religion as studied by anthropologists specifically, and social scientists generally, involves a two-step operation, according to Geertz. "First," he explains, "an analysis of the system of meanings embodied in the symbols which make up the religion proper, and second, the relating of these systems to social-structural and psychological process." Geertz has consistently demonstrated a receptiveness to the various disciplinary approaches to religious studies, including phenomenology as the study of "religion proper," and has suggested a model for multi-disciplinary complementarity. Here is a point which should capture the attention of the scientific humanists working on the agenda of Huxley as they attempt to demonstrate the possibility of humanism embodying the fundamental ingredients of religion.

Anthropology is an interpretive science, says Geertz, which is engaged in the search for meaning through a systematic analysis of culture, i.e., the study of human meanings embodied in symbols. "The concept of culture I espouse," he continues, "is essentially a semiotic one. Analysis is sorting out the structures of significance and determining their ground and import." The concept of culture which Geertz is embracing denotes "an historically transmitted pattern of meanings embodied in symbols, a system of inherited conceptions expressed in symbolic forms by means of which men communicate, perpetuate, and develop their knowledge about and attitudes toward life." Here, then, is the core of Huxley's task and agenda, namely, to create a mechanism which experientially transmits patterns of meanings through the medium of symbols without the benefit of supernatural transcendence. This process elevates humanism to a religion with all of the essential ingredients. It will foster life and knowledge, based on experience and validated through scientific experimentation, while drawing attention to the human symbols of self-reliance and responsibility to the community and to the world.

If culture is the expression of meaning, and anthropology is the analysis of culture, we can say that the fundamental task of anthropology, put succinctly, is the systematic analysis of meaning. And this systematic analysis, or systematization of meaning, necessitates an analysis of the socio-cultural structures and processes which constitute the framework of meaning. This systems analysis approach implies interpretation, or, more correctly, hermeneutics. A humanistic hermeneutic is possible only if and when humanism can demonstrate the meaning and purpose of life through cultural symbols carrying both knowledge of the world and responsiveness to human emotions. If culture is the experience and expression of meaning (or, rather, the context within which, and the socio-historical mechanism whereby, meaning is both experienced and expressed), then the function of the concept of meaning necessarily is interpretive, or, if one prefers, hermeneutical, and in turn, anthropology constitutes the analytical mechanism for identifying and systematizing meaning such that it serves as an effective interpretation of human culture. In other words, *culture is meaning* and *meaning is hermeneutics*.

An essential quality of the anthropological enterprise is its desire for universal application. The cross-cultural perspective is the *sine qua non* of anthropological method. The same might likewise be said of Huxley's humanism in that it must be universal to be considered true and valuable at all for, in the absence of absolute universality, scientific knowledge is meaningless. The desired benefit in the employment of anthropological method is the facilitation of what Geertz has called "the enlargement of the universe of human discourse." Anthropology's sensitivity to the vast panorama of human experience, exemplified in a substantially built up collection of cross-cultural studies, plays a vital role in establishing the discipline's capacity to interpret meaning-systems. For, says Geertz, in any anthropological analysis of culture patterns, there is an attempt to observe and understand "the degree to which it is informed." The challenge here to humanism is clear — it must be universal and it must be understandable. And, by universal understanding we mean a capacity to interpret meaning-systems through the evolutionary scientific grid rather than through the grid of a supernatural reality comprised of a dualistic worldview with an intervening God. Unless humanism can do this, it will fail as a philosophy of life and as a religion without God.

We are confronted with three alternative responses to the anthropological approach to the analysis of culture and religion: (1) To be impressed with the dynamics of cultural diversity while vigorously pursuing the analysis of various culture forms and contents yet forgoing any philosophical speculation as to the implications of such an impression; (2) to be impressed with cultural diversity while concluding that life has no transcendent value and that the only absolute is "relativity," or (3) to be informed by cultural diversity as form-and-content expressions of meaning which are understood to be reflections of meaning-reality. The discipline of anthropology, when strictly adhering to its definition as a science for the systematic analysis of socio-cultural phenomena, is bound to the first option — observation, description, understanding, and interpretation. Nowhere is the discipline forced to adhere either to the second or third option and when it does, it either steps into the circle of positivism (in the second option) or philosophy (in the third option). Likewise with scientific humanism, namely, either it has the capacity to interpret the world within the context of its own reality without reference to transcendence, or it must give up the pursuit of constructing a meaning-system devoid of God.

We can most decidedly discount the second option from this discussion as antipathetic to the integrity of anthropology as a social science. The second option, where tenaciously held to, would result in anthropology's devolution to a mere ideological sect. From the very outset of this discussion, we have understood Geertz to be suggesting that anthropology, defined in terms of the first option, when engaged in a dialogue with philosophy could fruitfully lead to an interfacing of methods suggested in the third option — a method of religio-cultural analysis. Geertz is clear in his portrayal of the vocation of anthropology appropriate to this point:

> To look at the symbolic dimensions of social action — art, religion, ideology, science, law, morality, common sense — is not to turn away from the existential dilemmas of life for some empyrean realm of de-emotionalized forms; it is to plunge into the midst of them. The essential vocation of interpretive anthropology is not to answer our deepest questions, but to make available to us answers that others, guarding other sheep in other valleys, have given and thus to include them in the consultable record of what man has said. (Geertz, 1964).

Nowhere has Geertz or Huxley come closer together than on this point of a community of cross-cultural consultation, sharing, and exploration. With Geertz, this point focuses upon the data of anthropological research, whereas with Huxley it centers upon the scientific community's persistent, relentless, and uncompromising pursuit of truth through consultative experimentation and exploration. Scientific humanism intends to bring together the entire human effort of consultative knowledge in the quest for scientific understanding, an understanding brought about, not by an intervening God from outside, but by the collaborative effort of a rational community of scholars and scientists from inside the biosphere.

We need not attempt a resolution here of the age-old philosophical dispute over whether the presence of order is in the world, and thus *discoverable*, or whether order is in the mind, and thus *constructed*. The answer to such a problem, though certainly tantalizing, is not a prerequisite to our observation about humanity being driven to find/create order-system-category in the world. This drive is suggestive of an imperative in human experience — no society exists without a conception of order in the world or of system in experience. Within religious communities, suggests Geertz, sacred symbols function to synthesize that community's "worldview" (structure of reality — metaphysics) and its "ethos" (style of life — values).

The human drive to make sense out of experience, to impose upon it or find within it form and order, says Geertz, "is evidently as real and as pressing as the more familiar biological needs." This making "sense out of experience" is what we are calling here the systematics of meaning. It is a challenge and an opportunity, not just for traditional religious systems such as Christianity, Judaism, and Islam, but for scientific humanism as well. The making sense out of experience without reference to a transcendent intervening agent separates humanism from all theological systems of interpretation. It is to humanity, not to God, that humanists must look for the understanding and interpretation of meaning systems. "Men are congenitally compelled," says the sociologist Peter Berger, "to impose a meaningful order upon reality" (*The Sacred Canopy: Elements of a Sociological Theory of Religion*, NY: Anchor, 1969). Of course, this was said long ago by the pre-Socratics but Berger has brought the agenda of meaning-seeking back into the forefront of social science under the influence of Karl Mannheim. "One fundamental human trait which is of crucial importance in understanding man's religious enterprise," Berger says, "is his propensity for order." This drive, if religious, manifests itself more clearly in scientific research than in any other human endeavor and certainly more so than within the confines of a supernatural religious system vulnerable to traces of magic and superstition.

As we have seen, religion and culture are integrative expressions of meaning. We can further argue that science is the ultimate expression of meaning-seeking activity guided by reason and logic and serving the human community's quest for an enlightened view of the meaning and purpose of the world. There is, nevertheless, admittedly more to meaning than just its experientially-based expressions found in religious behavior and cultural artifacts. Humanity has always sought to organize our expressions of meaning and no society has ever been devoid of systematizers, as Paul Radin pointed out years ago. "There can be little doubt," he observed in his little classic, *Primitive Man as Philosopher* (NY: Dover, 1957), "that every group, no matter how small, has, from time immemorial, contained individuals who were constrained by their individual temperaments to occupy themselves with the basic problems of what we customarily term philosophy." As with philosophy, so with scientific effort, namely, our unabated effort to understand and interpret the meaning of life is the paramount human agenda. "Hence," says Geertz, "any scientific approach to the study of symbols (anthropology is essentially a refined science of symbolism) is interpretive by nature. It is a search for meaning which results in an explication of the symbol. In short, anthropological writings are themselves interpretations, and second and third order ones to boot."

In our investigation of the possibilities of interfacing anthropological analysis and religious behavior, Geertz's definition of anthropology as an "interpretive science" has given rise to a characterization of anthropology as the systematic analysis of *culture as meaning*. It can also be suggested that, in an attempt to understand religiously motivated behavior, the human propensity for order gives rise to an intellectual interest in the systematic analysis of *religion as meaning*. The social scientific approach to the study of religion, as demonstrated in Geertz, is a systematic analysis of the content and forms of religious and cultural phenomena. Geertz says anthropology does not seek to understand the "basis of belief" but rather "belief's manifestations," that is, ideology, myth, ritual, and symbols.

The task of analyzing and systematizing the "basis of belief" resides squarely in the lap of theologians and philosophers. If humanists are to have their rightful part in this systematization process, they must demonstrate that scientific knowledge can supply a viable "basis of belief" without the encumbering trappings in the physical world of supernatural intervention by a transcendent being. If humanists can show how the basis of belief in the meaning and direction of life can be found within, rather than outside, phenomenal reality, then the agenda is set. Purveyors of religious faith have contended all along that the only legitimate source and basis of belief is outside this world rather than inside it. Belief must be supernatural rather than natural. Belief must be external and alien rather than intrinsic and ubiquitous to the universe. For Huxley and most humanists of the modern period, the discovery of DNA and genetics, atomic theory, and the new physics give grounds for hope that religion as a meaning-system can be earth-based rather than heaven-based and intrinsic to the world rather than alien to it. Religion without God, rather than because of God, is the demonstration called for by Huxley and company. If a meaning-system can be established without dependence upon supernaturalism, then scientific humanism might just rightfully be called a *religion without God* whereby *humanism as spiritual journey* makes sense.

Human experience finds expression through the meaning-systems of culture and religion. The analysis of experientially stimulated meaning-expressions and the systematization of this analytic enterprise has occupied our time through these deliberations.

That we have defined religion and culture in terms of the category of experience must necessarily inform our definition of anthropology. More precisely, our effort is to nurture an anthropological method which is concentrated upon experiential meaning as the key to understanding both culture and religion. From this we can argue that both religion and culture are meaning-systems and meaning is hermeneutics, that is, an interpretational construct. Just as surely as culture is this-worldly yet a meaning-system, religion might likewise be described as a meaning-system based in this world rather than in a supernatural world if and when (and only if and when) the meaning-system which it embraces *resonates experientially* within the human community. It is experiential validation that humanists seek in their presentation of a godless religion, a religion drawing from scientific knowledge which itself fosters and nurtures awe, wonder, and reverence within the human heart.

Of course, the more jaded and crusty humanists among us marvel at the bother of defining humanism as a *religion without God*. It might be argued, and somewhat persuasively, that the bother is not worth the results, for the humanists already know what they know and the religious community is certain of its own position as well. It certainly could be argued that "all argumentation with presupposition is circular," and, thus, the humanists end up where they started out, as do the faithful. To employ traditionally sacrosanct nomenclature such as "religion," "God," "Divinity," "awe," "reverence," "wonder," and the like, while providing each one with a humanistic rather than theistic meaning not only does not move dialogue forward but seems dangerously close to actually contributing to its ineffectiveness. If we cannot agree on the meaning of the words we use, then how can we ever come to an understanding, to say nothing of an agreement, on these issues?

Still and all, the warm-blooded humanists who so desperately desire to free religiously trapped people from their shackles can hardly resist proposing the use of the old language with new meaning, or, more precisely, with a deeper and more reflective understanding of our present reality. For those who deeply experience awe, wonder, and reverence in the world about them, in themselves, and in their encounters with others, the yearning for a validation of that experience is real and legitimate. Yet, many of these same individuals find themselves disenfranchised from the religious establishment for refusing to embrace a pre-modern notion of an interventionist God, a God of the Bible, who consistently exhibits primitive, irrational and erratic behavior. The Garden of Eden, the flood, parting of water and stopping the sun, blood sacrifice of the son to appease the anger of the father God, the virgin birth of a God/Man, the Son who is his own Faterh by virtue of incest with his own mother, and eternal damnation by fire — all of these things fly in the face of reason and modern science. However, the experience of awe, wonder, and reverence still persists, even grow, in the midst of a deepening understanding of the evolutionary process of creation. Is there not a legitimate place for such as these in the world?

*Adapted from my book, *IN THE ABSENCE OF GOD: Religious Humanism as Spiritual Journey (with special reference to Sir Julian Huxley)*.

Notes

Primary sources by Sir Julian Huxley used in this paper.

Religion Without Revelation (1927 and 1957)

Knowledge, Morality, and Destiny (1960)

Julian Huxley: Scientist and World Citizen (1975)

Julian Huxley: Memories (1970)

Evolutionary Humanism (1958)

Secondary sources consulted in this paper.

Berger, Peter (1967), *The Sacred Canopy: Elements of a Sociological Theory of Religion* (NY: Dover Publ.).

Clark, Ronald W. (1986). *The Huxleys* (London: Oxford University Press).

Eastman, Roger (1975), "Is Secular Humanism a Religion?," in *The Way of Religion* (NY: Harper & Row).

Geertz, Clifford (1966), "Religion as a Cultural System" in Michael Banton, Editor, *Anthropological Approaches to the Study of Religion* (London: Tavistock Publ.).

Hutcheon, Pat Duffy (1999), "Julian Huxley: From Materialism to Evolutionary Naturalism," *Humanist in Canada*, Autumn.

Madigan, Timothy J. (2002), "Evolutionary Humanism Revisited: The Continuing Relevance of Julian Huxley," *American Humanist Association*.

Morgan, John. H. (2005), *Naturally Good: The Behavioral History of Moral Development (from Charles Darwin to E. O. Wilson),* (South Bend, IN: Cloverdale Books).

Morgan, John H. (2006), *Being Human: Perspectives in Meaning and Interpretation (Essays in Religion, Culture, and Personality) Second Edition,* (South Bend, IN: Quill Books).

Morgan, John H. (2006), "Ethical Humanism and the 'New Divinity': Exploring Post-Biblical Religion In a Secular World, or How to Spell 'Spiritual Relief'," lecture presented at the 2006 Summer Programme in Theology at Oxford University.

Morgan, John H. (2007), *IN THE ABSENCE OF GOD: Religious Humanism as Spiritual Journey (with special reference to Sir Julian Huxley)* (South Bend, IN: Cloverdale Books).

Morgan, John H. (2007), *"IN THE BEGINNING...": The Paleolithic Origins of Religious Consciousness* (South Bend, IN: Cloverdale Books, 2007).

Radin, Paul (1957), *Primitive Man as Philosopher* (NY: Dover Publ.).

Pope Benedict XVI on Islam: Setting the Stage for a Culture of Dialogue

Bernard J. O'Connor

The appointment of Cardinal Jean-Louis Tauran in June, 2007, as President of the Pontifical Council for Interreligious Dialogue is generally considered to be a sign of Pope Benedict's "commitment to dialogue with Muslims." During the previous year the Council had been merged with that of Culture under the presidency of Cardinal Paul Poupard. Cardinal Tauran has clarified: By once again separating both Councils, Interreligious Dialogue not only "recovers its autonomy," but acquires the potential to become "a more effective instrument in the service of dialogue among religions."

Few may be aware that the move to unite the two Councils had not been especially well received within the Islamic world. In November 2006, the Pope met with Mustapha Cherif, "an expert on Islam at the University of Algiers." Professor Cherif voiced disappointment concerning the Holy Father's having appointed the same Cardinal to head both Councils. This decision, he said, could be interpreted "as a lack of sensitivity to interreligious dialogue" because of "lessening the weight and identity of that Vatican dicastery."[1]

It is difficult to assume that Professor Cherif's critique was the dominant factor in prompting Pope Benedict to revise his prior decision. But apparently the Pope took seriously his and other objections and so the Council for Interreligious Dialogue has been reinstated. The message is clear. The Pontiff listens, attentively and critically. And he shows humility and prudence in being able to admit that there are times when one must reassess and even reverse previous policies. The Church's involvement with Islam is such an important priority for Pope Benedict that he is willing to take whatever measures are necessary in order to advance their relationship.

Theme

The following study will consider how Pope Benedict perceives and approaches Islam and its adherents.

This analysis will center around his advocacy of "dialogue." The term recurs consistently throughout the Pope's discourse since his election on April 19, 2005. For example, in his Address to the Diplomatic Corps in Ankara, Turkey, on November 28, 2006, he referred to dialogue four times in a brief span of thirteen paragraphs. The significance of such usage is that it reliably exhibits the Pope's attitude toward Islam. His appeal to dialogue is now widely regarded as being indicative of a core thrust of his pontificate. The Cardinal Prefect of the Vatican's Congregation for Sainthood Causes once characterized the Pope's stance by stating that "dialogue with Islam is an obligation for the Church", a preferred means of constructive engagement. It must be said, however, as has the personal secretary of Pope Benedict, Msgr. Georg Gaenswein, that there is no single "voice that ties all Muslims together and leads them. There are many different currents," often in formidable opposition to each other.[2]

Nor is the nature of dialogue in this as in any other context entirely self-evident. Literature abounds on the subject of what constitutes dialogue, especially in the areas of Political Science, Conflict Management and Law. Kimberlee Kovach's, *Mediation:*

Principles and Practice, typifies the *genre*. According to Kovach, dialogue is associated with negotiation and presumes an openness to communicate.

Dialogue is an aspect of the process by which to identify and resolve divisive issues, so that parties may ultimately reduce their losses and possibly even emerge with an improved relationship. The purpose is to overcome differences and to diminish their negative consequences. A result of dialogue in mediation has often been described as 'Win-Win'. This definitely suggests what the Pope has in mind with his endorsement of dialogue. For instance, in his Address to the Ambassador of Turkey on January 19, 2007, Pope Benedict demonstrated both familiarity with, and respect for, third-party intervention as a method to assist with "the resumption of negotiations", where these have lapsed into *impasse*. Improved "rapprochement" is prone to yield conspicuous and concrete benefits; all favorable to enhancing "dialogue between Religious Authorities at all levels."[3]

But experts like Kovach, though believing in flexibility, tend to leave little to chance. Entering into negotiation requires nurturing an intent among participants which is conducive, along with acquiring competent and impartial third-party interveners, and creating an ambience which is suitable for such an exacting interaction to take place. There is then a sense in which various principles and prerequisites are formally incorporated so as to achieve a culture of dialogue. To ignore them would be to risk the collapse of subsequent efforts at dialogue and be left with the demise of hopes for a conciliated coexistence.

When one examines the multiple references to Islam offered by Pope Benedict, knowing that he strongly espouses the cause of dialogue, it may be noted that his statements actually imply pro-dialogue 'conditions'. For they express what is necessary in order for a deeper and more profound 'conversation' with Islam to occur. The Pope's remarks, whether or not always conscious of this explicit dynamic, nevertheless collectively contribute to the formation of a pro-dialogue mindset. When such is successful in being transmitted and received, successive steps in conventional negotiation may proceed where and when deemed feasible.

Conciliar Background

Speaking to a special assembly of Muslim representatives on September 25, 2006, the Pope said that he was "placing (himself) firmly within this perspective," namely that of Vatican II's Declaration on the Relationship of the Church to Non-Christian Religions, *Nostra Aetate*.[4] His speeches, letters, etc. regularly quote its Articles as well as passages from the Council's Constitution on the Church, *Lumen Gentium*.[5] The wisdom of the Council Fathers provides the essential background for Pope Benedict's views on Islam as well as grounds the 'pro-dialogue' reality.

What did the Council teach about Islam?

Islam is described in *Lumen Gentium* 16 as holding "the first place" among those "who, professing the faith of Abraham, along with us adore the one and merciful God, who on the last day will judge mankind." We share a spiritual kinship through Abraham. We each teach God's mercy and compassion, and we believe that humanity is accountable before God. Number 841 of the *Catechism of the Catholic Church*, by quoting LG 16, reinforces the Article's validity.

Nostra Aetate 3 emphasizes that the Church "looks with esteem" to Islam. The Article elaborates upon LG 16. We similarly "adore God," Who is "living and enduring, merciful and all powerful, Maker of heaven and earth and Speaker to men." Islam seeks "to submit wholeheartedly even to His inscrutable decrees." And Islam, though not subscribing to the doctrine of Jesus' divinity within the Trinity, does "revere Him as a prophet." Islam also "honors Mary, His virgin mother." And because of a certainty in the Day of Judgment, Muslims "prize the moral life, and give worship to God especially through prayer, almsgiving and fasting."

Despite those "many quarrels and hostilities" which have arisen throughout history between Christians and Muslims, the Council "urges all" to progress beyond that past and "to strive sincerely for mutual understanding." Before "all mankind," together we must "make common cause of safeguarding and fostering social justice, moral values, peace and freedom."

On the Fortieth Anniversary of *Nostra Aetate*, the President of the Mufti Council of Russia stated: "For the first time in the history of Christian-Muslim relations, the Church saw in Muslims not enemies or heretics, but participants with equality of rights in relations between humanity." The Declaration "laid the basis for reciprocal cooperation between Catholics and Muslims on a world scale." [6]

The Culture of Dialogue

At least five elements of 'pro-dialogue conditions' are discernible in the thought of Pope Benedict on Islam. Together they allow the Church to witness to a "new season of dialogue and spiritual solidarity" with Islam, as with "the other great religious traditions."[7] For the culture of dialogue to evolve and mature, setting the stage for dialogue must recognize that:

(a) *The parties accept each other, a sign of hope for the waiting world.* Acceptance between the parties is an announcement to the world. On numerous occasions Pope Benedict has stated unequivocally that he has "esteem and profound respect for Muslim believers." He often portrays them as "dear and esteemed Muslim friends." And he emphasizes that his personal conviction reflects the favorable attitude seen in *Nostra Aetate* 3. On the part of Islam, soon after the Pope's election, the President of the Central Council of Muslims in Germany credited him with having "contributed much to opening the priority" of Catholic-Muslim dialogue promoted by Pope John Paul II. The Imam of Rome's Grand Mosque was equally laudatory of Pope Benedict, saying that he "follows a line of continuity in relation to Muslims."[8]

The Pope reminds us that the world has a stake in observing "harmonious relations between Christian and Muslim communities." This is because "all people are linked by profound solidarity, and must be encouraged" to assess differences so as not to justify confrontation, but "to foster mutual respect." The "world looks….in hopeful expectation." This should motivate our subsequent dialogue. This should also motivate us to embark upon dialogue by "refusing generalization in judging people." We are to greet each other with an accessible mind and heart. And we must therefore jointly affirm that "objective morality" is crucial to our commitment to "a proper respect for life and for the dignity of every human person."[9]

(b) *There is mutual benefit in the quest for "authentic reciprocal knowledge."*
Whether dialogue pertains to the interreligious or inter-cultural arenas, participants are guided by the realization that they "must learn to know one another better." That learning mode may be diverse, which is why the Turkish Embassy sponsored a "show for whirling dervishes from Konya." The performance by "these mystical dancers, typical in Sufism," was held in the Vatican's Chancery Palace, and as a tribute to "music and dance (being) universal languages."[10]

The Pope has remarked, with reference to the country of Chad, that "relations between Christians and Muslims are generally good," and that this is due "in particular to the pursuit of better mutual knowledge." This in turn becomes the catalyst for other collaborative initiatives. It also permits us to assert that dialogue presumes and "requires reciprocity." For example, the Christian community "must live the commandment of love taught by Christ," embracing immigrants in that spirit, while "Christians living in Islamic countries "should also be received well, and with respect for their religious identity."

Montenegro similarly illustrates that Christian-Muslim encounter may lead to "outstanding examples" of advantages for both traditions. Likewise, during a visit to the Pope by the President of the Republic of Sudan on September 14, 2007, the topics discussed included how interreligious dialogue not only stimulates active collaboration but elicits "the promotion of peace and the common good." Among the implications of dialogue is to validate that commonality is inherent "between cultures and religions." What we share strengthens our capacity to confront those numerous "challenges we all face regarding the family and society."[11]

(c) *Progress in dialogue is achieved incrementally.*
The Pope has applauded those instances in which Christians and Muslims strive "to work together" in a gradual yet systematic movement involving "many common undertakings." He may well have anticipated projects like that of "shared pilgrimages." The Way of Mary organization, for example, provides a network by which to facilitate meetings and thematic trips. There is also the opportunity at such airports as Heathrow in London to designate "the same multi-religious place of prayer" for passengers in transit.

The betterment of local and international cooperation is always encouraged by Pope Benedict. This is part of the rationale for why "a common accord to establish diplomatic relations" was agreed upon in May 2007, between the Holy See and the United Arab Emirates. The Pope is aware, too, of the Catholic-Muslim educational program in Morocco, "comprising 15 schools with 12,000 Muslim students (and) in which the Koran is taught," under the authority of the Catholic bishop.

Moreover, in the annual Message to Muslims (2007) to commemorate the conclusion of Ramadan, the Pontifical Council for Interreligious Dialogue supported Pope Benedict's outlook by emphasizing that an ongoing "intensification" is foremost in "the pursuit of dialogue between Christians and Muslims." In other words, such aspirations as to ensure "that the younger generations" do not become "blocs opposed to one another," come to pass when sequential steps unfold logically and deliberately. "Dialogue" thus becomes a viable "tool which can help us" to surpass the "multiple tensions" habitually afflicting us.[12]

The overall picture, however, is not wholly optimistic, as with the status of rights for religious minorities in Turkey. This prompted Vatican and Turkish representatives "at the time of Benedict XVI's visit" to discuss "the possibility of establishing a 'mixed working group' to resolve" problems which beset the Church. The proposal is yet to be implemented, but has been brought forward.

Although there are obstacles, Judaism, Christianity and Islam are still "called to cooperate with one another" on behalf of humanity. Their "genuine dialogue" is expressed in explicit "acts of human solidarity." And "cruel fanaticism may not be allowed to poison (these) relations."[13]

(d) *The lessons of history speak to rationality.*
Pope Benedict's lecture at the University of Regensburg on September 12, 2006, aroused something of a furor. But closer examination of his remarks reveals that he was definitely not repudiating either his own or the Church's regard for Islam. As might be surmised, media hype and its 'spin' on the text inflamed delicate sensibilities. By contrast, the Pope dealt with the research of Munster's Professor Theodore Khoury as it related to a Fourteenth Century 'dialogue' between "Byzantine emperor Michael II Paleologus and an educated Persian," an adherent of Islam. At the crux of their debate was the issue that "not to act in accordance with reason is contrary to God's nature." The interpretation of reason from the Greek philosophical perspective (Paleologus) would seem at first sight to differ radically from the "Muslim teaching, that God is not bound up with any of our categories, even that of rationality." There are, of course, possible implications for enforced conversion and for the idea that

"violence is incompatible with the nature of God and of the soul." The Pope was not degrading, and indeed defends, belief in "God's transcendence and otherness." There is credible scholarship which corroborates. As one authority on Islamic-Christian dialogue, Maurice Borrmans, remarked: "The Pope wished to teach that faith is not irrational." And it now falls to us "to take up dialogue again" and among its themes to address "the meaning of history, and the sacredness of creation."

James V. Schall agrees. Reginsburg is a reminder that "Islamic philosophy and Western philosophy, not to mention Eastern philosophy, often had similar intellectual roots and presuppositions. This is why it is not correct to view this lecture as simply concerned with Islam." The Pope aptly declares that, "the exaltation of man by revelation does not imply that he is not what he is created to be, a rational animal, one who does all he does by 'logos', by reason."

Pope Benedict's approach to reason was critiqued in an Open Letter signed by 38 Islamic experts in 2006. They stated that the dichotomy between faith and reason as understood by the Pontiff "does not exist in precisely the same form" for Islam. "Reason itself is one among the many signs within us, which God invites us to contemplate …. as a way of knowing the truth." While this may seem to be a point of notable difference, Schall's evaluation verifies that said difference is not an impediment to discussion.

Pope Benedict regularly extols "the remarkable flowering of Islamic civilization" which is disclosed in the "glorious past" of nations such as Turkey. History attests, as in the case of Pope Gregory VII (1076), that despite how Christians and Muslims profess belief in God "in a different manner," they continue to "owe charity" to one another.

Charity, expressed as love of God and love of neighbor, is the primary thrust of a second Open Letter to Pope Benedict, issued on October 13, 2007, and with 138 signatories from among Muslim Religious leaders. They chose to accentuate "the common word between us and you." The Pope replied by speaking of his "deep appreciation for this gesture," and by inviting a delegation of those who signed the Letter to meet with him. For Pope Benedict, this Letter is a reaffirmation of "the importance of dialogue based on effective respect for the dignity of the person," and "on objective knowledge of the other's religion."[14]

(e) *Dialogue anticipates that truth will be spoken with sensitivity and courage.*
In his Angelus message of September 17, 2006, Pope Benedict stated that he was "deeply sorry for the reactions" generated in "some countries" to his Regensburg lecture. He explained that his words "in their totality" were an "invitation to (a) dialogue" which is meant to be "frank and sincere, with great mutual respect." Some, including Bishop L. Padovese, the Apostolic Vicar of Anatolia, are of the opinion that such candor is not always welcome in Muslim circles, since there are Muslims who are adamant in their "absolutism" to an extent which "does not allow for .... dialogue or compromise." While "a gathering of information" and its dissemination is possible, "this isn't genuine dialogue."

Justo L. Balda of the Missionaries of Africa, a scholar of Islam, considers that the "binomial faith and reason" orientation of the Pope is "most difficult and conflictive" for Muslims, but need not escalate to any "cynicism in the religious field, (itself) a dangerous cancer of our time." Cardinal Cormac Murphy-O'Connor summarized Pope Benedict's position when he told the Muslim Council of Wales that dialogue should be so guided by truth that "dialogue becomes fruitful only when everyone involved feels able to say what he or she believes, or what identifies him or her as a Muslim or as a Christian."

The Cardinal's propensity for directness mirrors that of the Holy Father himself, who informed journalists on July 25, 2005, that Islam "certainly has elements that could make peace prevail; (yet) it also has other elements. We must always try to identify the best elements." But we must shun superficiality. Gregorian University Professor, Ilaria Morali, advises that there are Muslim academics who think that "dialogue" has "become an expression that has suffered inflation, as it is used without coming to the point." There are Muslims who presume that dialogue merely amounts to "gestures of friendship and solidarity, avoiding a serene but difficult confrontation including on painful" issues. She continues: "dialogue cannot be improvised; (and) it is a mistake to conceive it 'solely' in the abstract." She has captured the essence of Pope Benedict's approach.

Professor Morali has also touched upon a concern articulated in 1999 by the international Islamic-Catholic Committee when that Committee stated: "In order to build a culture of dialogue it is important to have clarity on the nature of dialogue. It covers all forms of encounter which promote mutual understanding." What the second Open Letter manifests is a bid for precisely this clarity. The signal communicated is: "We still want to talk to you – and to other Christian leaders too." The Muslim authors thereby also parallel the Holy See's latest attempts at bringing about "a new relationship with Islam, one that combines theology with what it calls an 'ethical dialogue' – in other words, a conversation about shared values."[15]

Conclusion

When Pope Paul VI defined 'dialogue' for Catholic ecclesiology, he said that "it has many forms. If necessary it takes account of actual experience. It chooses appropriate means (and) it does not hold fast to forms of expression." (16) This essay's application to dialogue based upon the principles and methods of modern Peace Studies and Alternative Dispute Resolution is one of those "many forms": one with resiliency and malleability. And it permits us to contextualize Pope Benedict's esteem for Islam in terms of a pro-dialogue disposition which prevents the culture of dialogue from becoming entrenched or restricted. An old Chinese proverb is fitting: No bird builds a nest in a bare tree. From the preceding discussion, we may further conclude that:

(i) *Peace is the ultimate goal of the "common task of reflection" for action.*
The Pope maintains that "trusting dialogue" is not entered into as an end in itself. Instead, it must give rise to "the practical expression of our common willingness to help (each other) to (fulfill a) legitimate aspiration to live in justice and peace." Dialogue, of whatever variety and in whatever phase, "begins in daily life." And it "must start by denouncing violence," especially that manipulating "the pretext of religious motivations." Protection of "fundamental" human rights, which is to say those derived from our pervasive longing for security and peace, properly evokes the attention of Christians and Muslims, and whom LG 16 designates as being progeny of "the Patriarch Abraham."

But protection must not disguise itself as an "imposition of outside values and culture." Indeed, focus groups held in Morocco, Lebanon, and Jordan, argue that what is perceived as imposition by Islamist political parties will always arouse their vigorous resistance. Even among the proponents of a primarily secular governance model, there is scant regard for those parties which are considered to "too quick(ly) .... create alliances with external forces." Moderate Islamist parties "that reject violence and practice democratic ideals" do not disqualify the "place of Islam in public life." That place, however defined, must be determined by Muslims themselves, and by recourse to their own proper norms, tenets and heritage. Pope Benedict decidedly concurs.[17]

(ii) *Dialogue is "not an optional extra."*
With these words the Pope addressed representatives of Muslim communities in Cologne on August 20, 2005. He implied that making dialogue 'optional' amounts to an erroneous combination

of reductionism and minimalism. For these assault the "fact" that dialogue is "a vital necessity on which in large measure our future depends." And our efforts are sustained when we realize that "in many ways the Koran encourages dialogue with Jews and Christians." Therefore, Pope Benedict frequently refers to God in language intended to resonate with the Koran's invocation of "Allah, the Most Merciful." When assessing his Turkish visit, he stated: "I turned to the only Lord of heaven and earth, merciful Father of the whole of humanity."[18]

(iii) *The autonomy of the State need not degrade freedom of religion.* When meeting with the President of Turkey's Religious Affairs Directorate, Pope Benedict stressed that the Church, "while respecting the legitimate autonomy of temporal affairs, has a specific contribution to offer in the search for proper solutions to …. pressing questions." The Islamic State knows, too, of "legitimate independence from Shariah," the Islamic law. And so there is basis for Muslims and Christians at least to be able to discuss policies and legislation which target religious minorities, for example: Pakistan's Blasphemy Law, or the "1985 registration of Nigeria by the military government as an Islamic State," despite Christian protest, or the arrest of Christians in Saudi Arabia, where "only Islam is allowed public expression."

It is secularization, however, which undermines Islam and Christianity and which both religions must counter. This, therefore, should inspire them to respond directly, cooperatively and positively. When on November 6, 2007, "for the first time in history," the Saudi Arabian King visited the Holy See, the exchange with Pope Benedict centered upon "the importance of collaboration between Christians, Muslims and Jews." Although the problematic matter of the "more than 1 million Christians" residing in the Arabian peninsula was only "discreetly mentioned" by the Pope, the King's "stop at the Vatican" was still a remarkable tribute to the desire of "knowing each other better." Federico Lombardi, S.J., of the

Vatican Press Office, commented succinctly: "If we do not begin, we will never arrive."[19]

Although there is a valid "distinction between civil and religious dialogue," the two polarities convey that it remains vital "to accompany the dialogue partner in the process."[20] Pope Benedict's appreciation of Islam and his love for Muslims means that they shall never walk alone. Because he is dedicated "to accompany" them as a brother and as a fellow pilgrim of faith.

Notes

1. One may compare the statements of Cardinal Tauran with those of Professor Cherif. See the online Zenit News Service for June 26, 2007, Protocol No. ZE07062605, "Cardinal: Pope Shows Zeal for Dialogue." See also "Benedict XVI Meets with Muslim Philosopher," Zenit for November 13, 2006, ZE06111302. Hereafter, when Zenit is cited the reference will include only the date and Protocol. The Zenit web site is: www.zenit.org .

2. The text of the Pope's Address to the Diplomatic Corps in Ankara, Turkey, on November 28, 2006, is available at ZE06112808; while that of "Dialogue with Islam Seen as Obligation," is found at ZE06032404, March 24, 2006.
    Msgr. Gaenswein expressed this caution in an interview, "I Promise You My Fidelity." The interview, conducted by Peter Seewald, is featured in *Inside the Vatican*, Vol 15, No. 8, October, 2007. This citation is referred to on p. 42.

3. Kimberlee Kovach, *Mediation: Principles and Practice*, (St. Paul, MN: Thomson-West), 2004. Chapters 2 and 8 present the negotiation process. Pope Benedict's awareness of third-party intervention, relevant for what is described by Kovach, is noted in: Address to the Ambassador of Turkey to the Holy See, January 19, 2007, paragraphs 11, 13 and 14. The full text of the Address is available through the Vatican web site (www.vatican.va). Hereafter, whenever only the title and date of a Papal Address are given, the reference is to this site.

4   See Address to the Ambassadors of Countries with a Muslim Majority and to the Representatives of Muslim Communities in Italy, September 25, 2006, para. 2.

5   The translation of *Lumen Gentium* 16 and of *Nostra Aetate* 3 is that of Walter M. Abbott, editor of *The Documents of Vatican II*, (New York: Guild Press), 1966.

6   The comments of the President of Russia's Mufti Council are cited in "First Catholic-Muslim Conference in Russia Meets," November 27, 2005, ZE05112727.

7   The importance of a "new season of dialogue and spiritual solidarity" was mentioned by the Pope in his General Audience message of August 24, 2005, para. 15. The context was the Fortieth Anniversary of Vatican II's Declaration, *Nostra Aetate*.

8   The phrase pertaining to "esteem and profound respect" is often repeated. For example, see para. 2 of the Address to Ambassadors of Countries with a Muslim Majority, ibid. The variant usage of "dear and esteemed Muslim friends" is noted by a Consultor to the Pontifical Council for Interreligious Dialogue, Daniel Madigan, in "Benedict XVI and Catholic-Muslim Relations," September 16, 2005, ZE05091603, reply to Question one. That the Pope upholds *Nostra Aetate* is indicated in the Statement by Cardinal Tarcisio Bertone, September 16, 2006, para. 2.

The response of Central Council President, Nadeem Elyas, was featured in "World Reactions to Papal Election," April 23, 2005, ZE05042305. The comment by Rome's Imam is found in "Islam's Teachings Prohibit Terrorism," September 22, 2005, ZE05092201.

9   The "world looks," and is entitled to do so, the Pope told the Ambassador of Syria on December 14, 2006, para. 2 and 4. The avoidance of destructive generalization is therefore necessary. See the Islamic-Catholic Join Statement, March 8, 2004, ZE04030804, para. 3-4. The same must be said of our belief in "objective morality." Refer to, "Pope Lists Two Keys for World Peace," November 8, 2005, ZE05110807.

10 The importance of shared learning was stated by the Pope in his Address to the Ambassador of Turkey, summarized as, "Peace calls for Cooperation," January 19, 2007, ZE07011904. The Embassy later presented the Whirling Dervishes. See "Vatican hosts Whirling Dervishes Show," June 12, 2007, ZE07061204.

11 The Pope spoke of "better mutual knowledge" in his Address to the Episcopal Conference of Chad on their 'Ad Limina', September 23, 2006.

Refer to, "Pope Presents Keys for Christian-Muslim Dialogue," October 3, 2006, ZE06100306.

The Pope's emphasis upon reciprocity was noted by Archbishop G. Lajolo (Secretariat of State) in, "Vatican Unease over Islamic Countries," May 27, 2006, ZE06052701.

When accepting the credentials of the first Ambassador of Montenegro to the Holy See on January 22, 2007, the Pope paid tribute to the Christian-Muslim shared experience. See para. 9.

The topics on the agenda for the visit of the Sudanese President are mentioned in, "Benedict XVI Receives the President of Sudan," Vatican Information Service, No. VIS 070914 (260).

The relationship between dialogue and challenges posed with regards to family and society is recalled by Pope Benedict in his annual New Year Address to the Diplomatic Corps, January 8, 2007, para. 8.

12 "Common undertakings" are spoken of by the Pope in his Address to Ambassadors of Countries with a Muslim Majority, ibid.

The Way of Mary movement and the Civil Aviation Apostolate at Heathrow are discussed in the Final Document of the XVII Plenary Session of the Pontifical Council for the Pastoral Care of Migrants and Itinerant People, May 15-17, 2006, pp. 5-6.

"Strengthening international cooperation" is cited in, "Holy See and Arab State Establish Relations," May 31, 2007, ZE07053101; while Archbishop Landel of Rabat relates the success of the educational experience in, "Morocco: Where Christians and Muslims Get Along," January 21, 2005, reply to Question two.

For the Ramadan Message, issued on September 28, 2007, refer to the Vatican Information Service, No. VIS 070928 (540).

13 The proposal of "mixed working groups" is outlined in John Flynn's, "Christianity on Trial in Turkey," April 30, 2007, ZE07043029.

The Pope's plea to the "three monotheistic religions" was stated in his Address to the Members of the American Jewish Committee, March 16, 2006.

The threat of "cruel fanaticism" to Islamic-Christian relations was a topic during the private audience with Abdullah II. See, "Pope and King of Jordan Discuss Religious Freedom," September 12, 2005, ZE05091203.

14 The September 12, 2006, lecture at the University of Regensburg shows how the issue of faith and reason has preoccupied Christian and Islamic scholarship in one form or another for centuries, though perhaps analyzed

from a different starting point. The appraisal of Maurice Borrmans on reaction to the Regensburg lecture is discussed in, "Scholar Notes Positive Response to Regensburg Speech," January 30, 2007, ZE07013028.

The remarks of James V. Schall are stated in his interview, "Reginsburg Revisited," conducted by Carrie Gress. Refer to 'Zenit.org' for October 9, 2007, pp. 8 and 13. Schall's assessment may be compared to the 2006 Open Letter to His Holiness Pope Benedict XVI. Refer to the section entitled, "The Use of Reason."

Pope Benedict's appreciation of Islamic history and civilization and of the counsel of Pope Gregory VII are presented in his Address to the Religious Affairs Directorate of Turkey, November 28, 2006, para. 5, 6 and 13.

The Pope's response to the 2007 Letter is summarized in, "Benedict XVI Thanks Muslims for Letter," November 29, 2007, ZE07112902.

15 Refer to Angelus, September 17, 2006, para. 1

Bishop L. Padovese has doubts about the feasibility of dialogue, as stated in, "Pope's Visit to Turkey: a Unique Opportunity?," September 26, 2006, ZE06092601, Question eight. Justo Balda is cautious but relatively optimistic in his interview, "On Benedict XVI's Dialogue with Islam," November 19, 2006, ZE06111903, Question three. Cardinal Cormac Murphy-O'Connor associates dialogue with candor and truth in his Address to Muslim Council, June 16, 2007, ZE07061601, page 5.

The Pope spoke to journalists assembled at Introd, Italy, on July 25, 2005. See "Benedict's Top 15 Words," July 27, 2005, ZE05072704.

The interview with Professor Ilaria Morali is entitled, "The Demands of Dialogue with Muslims," November 29, 2006, ZE06112921, Questions two and three.

The Committee Report for the sessions conducted in Paris between July 1-3, 1999, is presented in: http://212.77.1.245/news_services/bulletin/news/5264.php?index=5264&po_date=12.07.1999

Parallelism between the approach of the signers of the 2007 Open Letter and that of the Holy See is noted in, "Table Talk for Monotheists," *The Economist*, October 13, 2007, p. 67.

16 Refer to Article 85 of Pope Paul VI's Encyclical, *Ecclesiam Suam*, August 6, 1964.

Article 64 provides a definition of dialogue which is quite generic, theoretical and broad; so much so that extending its 'umbrella' usage to today may result in the kind of frustration among some Muslim scholars which Professor Morali has encountered in Turkey. Pope Paul wrote: "To this internal drive of charity which seeks expression in the external gift of charity, we will apply the word 'dialogue'."

17 Peace emanates from "trusting dialogue." See Address to the Members of the Foundation for Interreligious and Intercultural Research and Dialogue, February 1, 2007, para. 6. That dialogue begins in "daily life" was stated to the Ambassador of Turkey, ibid, para. 11, as was the necessity of "denouncing violence," para. 9. The latter explains why the Holy See publicly declared its readiness "to mediate to save Nagaf, the Shiite holy city in Iraq." Refer to, "Holy See Willing to Mediate for Iraqi City," August 16, 2004. ZE04081603.

The affinity between peace and human rights among the offspring of Abraham was commented upon by the Pope in his General Audience for World Youth Day in Cologne, August 24, 2005, para. 15.

The findings of these focus groups are discussed by Leslie Campbell in, "Toward 'Normal Politics' in the Arab World." See *The Challenge of Islamists for EU and US Policies*, Muriel Asseburg and Daniel Brumberg (eds.), a joint SWP-Berlin and USIP Research Paper, November, 2007, page 68.

For an analysis of Moderate Islam's approach to "the place of Islam in public life," refer to Mona Yacoubian's, "Engaging Islamists and Promoting Democracy," a 2007 Special Report of the United States Institute of Peace (www.usip.org).

18 See Address to Meeting with Representatives of Some Muslim Communities in Cologne, August 20, 2005.

Sidney Griffith presents a two-part article, "A Look Inside the Koran and the Bible," July 26, 2004, ZE04072622, and July 27, 2004, ZE04072721. The quote is taken from Part 2, Question three.

The Pope's deliberate appeal to language suggestive of the Koran is noted in his evaluation of his Turkish trip, General Audience, December 6, 2006, ZE06120605, and in his Address to the Ambassador of Pakistan, June 1, 2007, ZE07060110, para. 6.

19 Address to President of Turkey's Religious Affairs Directorate, ibid, para. 11

The relationship between the State in Islam and Shariah law is discussed by David Forte in, "Islamic Law and its Democratic Potential," March 9, 2005, ZE05030923.

Pakistan's Blasphemy Law criminalizes "offenses against the Koran." See, "Pakistani Prelate Calls Blasphemy Law 'Unjust'," July 18, 2004, ZE04071807. The situation in Nigeria is noted in, "Islam Seen as Politicized in Nigeria," May 2, 2006, ZE06050201. See also, "7 Christians Released in Saudi Arabia," June 9, 2005, ZE05060906. Their release was "on condition they renounce private religious practice." A Saudi official has said, "that the kingdom would never allow churches to be built." Moreover, the unfortunate treatment of Christian converts in many Islamic countries is virtually legend. Refer to, "Freedom of Conscience and Islam," June 4, 2007, ZE07060408.

The visit of the Saudi King was reported widely in the media. Citations here are taken from, "Saudi King and Pope Discuss Need to Aid Families," November 6, 2007, ZE07110603, and "Saudi's Visit to Vatican Seen as Good Start," November 11, 2007, ZE07111107.

The possible relationship between the agenda of the King's visit and the second Open Letter is discussed by Wlodzimierz Redzioch in, "And With Muslims?," *Inside the Vatican*, Vol. 15, No. 10, December, 2007, pp. 15-18. Fulvio Scaglione develops the same theme in his editorial for Italy's *Avvenire*, November 7, 2007, p. 1. See, "Collaborazione Nei Valori Spirituali E Morali." Scaglione considers the visit to be highly relevant for the political situation of the Middle East.

The visit provoked a strong negative reaction from the Osama Bin Laden sector. See, "Al-Zawahiri Attacca Papa Benedetto," *Metro*, Rome, December 18, 2007, p. 6.

20 This is No. 13 of the "Conclusions and Recommendations" section of the Final Document of the XVII Plenary Session of the Pontifical Council of Migrants and Itinerant People, ibid.

Espiritualidad Masculina
Antonio Ramirez

Introducción

El tema de la espiritualidad es un tema sumamente actual, no solo en las iglesias y las sinagogas, pero sobre todo en el mundo "secular" y en las ciencias sociales. Los estudios de espiritualidad y psicología han ido en aumento. En las librerías se pueden ver filas de libros sobre temas de espiritualidad, religión, auto superación, meditación, etc.

La espiritualidad no es sinónimo de la religión. Aunque el termino religión bien entendido significa "re-ligar", es decir, re-conectar lo que se encuentra desintegrado, frecuentemente el termino religión se relaciona con algo institucional, doctrinal, formal, y muchas veces cultural. Estrictamente hablando, alguien puede ser muy espiritual sin pertenecer a alguna religión específica, y alguien puede pertenecer a alguna religión, sin tener una verdadera espiritualidad.

La espiritualidad es algo que nos conecta con algo mayor, con el non-ego, con algo trascendente, nosotros diríamos que nos conecta con Dios. La espiritualidad es algo que nos ayuda a ver de una nueva forma, nos hace estar presentes al presente, al ahora. Trae consigo paz, conciencia, empatía, amor, paz, sentido de la vida. Es como la respiración, es vida, es la Vida. La espiritualidad es también lo que da energía y pasión a la existencia.

Desde un punto de vista cristiano, la espiritualidad es una

forma de ver y tratar de imitar a la persona de Jesús. Diferentes espiritualidades se enfocan en diversos aspectos de Jesús y a partir de ese prisma se trata de identificar con El. Por ejemplo, la espiritualidad de la Cruz, inspirada por una señora laica mexicana de nombre Concepción Cabrera de Armida, se enfoca en Jesús como Sacerdote y Victima. Es en la Cruz donde Jesús se ofrece a sí mismo como la única ofrenda agradable al Padre, El es a la vez, Sacerdote y Victima. Esta espiritualidad busca infundir en sus seguidores la misma docilidad al Espíritu para ofrecerse junto con Jesús al Padre. Ser ofrenda permanente, como diría San Pablo en Romanos 12,1-2. La espiritualidad franciscana, por otro lado, busca imitar a Jesús en su pobreza y desprendimiento. Y así sucesivamente.

En este artículo vamos a hablar de la espiritualidad en general, y de la espiritualidad masculina en particular. Nos enfocaremos en como los varones pueden tener una vida de profundidad, de sensibilidad a lo Absoluto, de madurez, de responsabilidad personal, y de compasión. La espiritualidad masculina tiene como característica que es una espiritualidad de acción, pues al varón le gusta actuar y tratar de responder activamente a los problemas de la vida. Pero para actuar correctamente, se necesita ver correctamente. La contemplación, característica de toda verdadera espiritualidad, es algo que no le viene naturalmente al varón, sino que al contrario, el necesita ser enseñado o "iniciado" como veremos mas adelante.

Existen ciertos temas generales que se mencionan en mucha de la literatura sobre la espiritualidad masculina. Estos temas incluyen: los ritos de iniciación para varones, el verdadero y el falso yo, la acción y la contemplación, la muerte y la vida nueva, el duelo, el espacio liminal, el silencio, la naturaleza, el dolor, la herida del padre, y la necesidad de ancianos y mentores. Brevemente revisaremos estos temas como una sencilla introducción a la espiritualidad masculina.

Quizá lo más importante de este tema es lo que algunos autores llaman la transformación de la conciencia o iluminación. Para que pueda haber un cambio en la sociedad y en la forma en que nos relacionamos debe haber una conversión, transformación, cambio en nuestra percepción y en nuestra conciencia. Bíblicamente el termino de lo que hablamos es "metanoia", cambio de corazón, cambio de mente, y cambio de actitudes. Un termino en ingles que ayuda a comprender de que se trata esta transformación es "awareness". "Awareness" puede ser traducido de alguna forma como el "ser conciente", pero también puede ser entendido como "estar despierto", o "despertar" ("awake"). Una autentica espiritualidad lleva a un despertar y a un estar conciente de lo que es real e importante, y a un desprenderse de lo ilusorio que muchas veces es creado por el ego y por los valores de una sociedad materialista y consumista.

El proceso de iniciación de los varones es un proceso de muerte para el ego, muerte para el falso-yo, muerte de lo ilusorio, y un renacer y un despertar al verdadero yo, creado a imagen y semejanza de Dios. Es mas, el verdadero yo, participa de la divinidad, participa de Dios pues es templo del Espíritu Santo, como diría San Pablo. En este sentido, el renacer es el volver a tomar conciencia que somos uno en Dios, uno con todo lo que es, uno con la Vida.

Desgraciadamente la inocencia inicial se pierde a los pocos años de vida. Algo semejante a la salida del paraíso de Adán y Eva. Al salir de la inocencia donde todo es armonía (imagen del jardín), uno entra en lo que algunos llaman "complex-consciousness", algo así como conciencia compleja que se manifiesta en el pensamiento dualista. El pensamiento dualista tiene como característica la oposición y por lo tanto la competencia y muchas veces la agresión. Para defender lo propio se ataca al otro, especialmente al que se percibe como diferente o lo que amenaza a nuestro status-quo. Esta tendencia a culpar y buscar fuera de uno al enemigo es algo característico de la inmadurez, del falso yo, que se afirma al condenar y culpar al otro quien atenta contra la existencia del frágil ego.

Solo por lo que los cristianos llaman gracia es que uno vuelve a descubrir que la realidad no es binaria o dual, sino que es una, y esta realidad esta compuesta por lo que aparentemente es opuesto.

El ying-yang o al anima-animus es parte de toda espiritualidad o experiencia mística. Esta segunda inocencia es lo que podemos nombrar como iluminación o el despertar ("awakening"). Sin perder lo complejo de la experiencia humana, unos sabios y santos llegan a una segunda inocencia donde todo pertenece y donde no hay ya opuestos. Uno comienza a ver con el "tercer ojo" según algunas tradiciones orientales. O como diría Jesús, solo el que ha nacido de nuevo puede ver el Reino de Dios (Juan 3).

Espiritualidad Masculina

Como llega un niño, mas bien, un adolescente a ser un varón adulto? Y que significa ser un varón adulto? Quizás la pregunta más exacta es, que significa ser hombre? Es una pregunta que no se hace explícitamente. Por lo menos yo no recuerdo que esa pregunta se me haya hecho, o se haya reflexionado seriamente cuando crecía, ni después de muchos años de universidad y estudio. Se asume de alguna forma que todos los varones sabemos lo que significa ser un hombre. Pero, realmente sabemos?

Existen modelos culturales de lo que significa ser un hombre. Todos los conocemos: el "macho mexicano", el proveedor, el protector, el que no llora, el que pelea mucho, el que ha tenido muchas mujeres, o el que bebe más. Muchos vemos como estos modelos culturales han llevado a la opresión de la mujer y de los más débiles y ha llenado los libros de historia con guerras, tiranías, y corrupción.

Lo que es importante saber es que el adolescente no llega a ser hombre naturalmente, es decir, biológicamente. Es posible que físicamente parezca ser un adulto, pero psicológicamente, emocionalmente, espiritualmente no necesariamente es así. Es algo que las mujeres saben claramente. Muchas veces y desgraciadamente por lo general, el hombre es un adolescente interiormente y se comporta como tal. Se centra en si mismo, se pelea cuando las cosas no salen como el quiere, se guarda sus sentimientos y no los sabe expresar, quiere controlar y dominar, y vive con un gran temor. Según James Hollis, el hombre vive con ocho secretos y uno de ellos es que su vida esta gobernada por el temor.

Es por esta razón que en casi todas la culturas del mundo y por muchos siglos en diferentes zonas del planeta existían (en algunos lugares aun existen) los ritos de iniciación para los varones. Estos ritos son conducidos por los ancianos y sabios de la comunidad que ritualmente inician al joven para que llegue a ser un hombre al servicio de la comunidad. Desgraciadamente estos ritos de iniciación se perdieron en la cultura occidental y es solo hasta estos días que se están recuperando y volviendo a estudiar. El sacerdote norteamericano franciscano Richard Rohr llega a afirmar que la falta de iniciación del joven es quizás la razón principal de la falta de madurez en el liderazgo político y religioso en los Estados Unidos. Y si revisamos la historia política y religiosa de Latino América, vemos claramente la falta de madurez y sabiduría en nuestros lideres. Tan solo falta ver los debates políticos y las declaraciones de muchos líderes religiosos en nuestros países.

Ritos de Iniciación

El tema central de la iniciación es la muerte del "ego" y el nacimiento o descubrimiento del verdadero yo. Jesús dice: "Si el grano de trigo no cae en tierra y muere, queda solo, pero si muere da mucho fruto" También leemos en los evangelios que "Hay que morir para vivir". El misterio central de la fe cristiana es lo que se conoce como el Misterio Pascual: "Cristo ha muerto, Cristo ha resucitado, Cristo vendrá otra vez". Jesús es el modelo por excelencia de lo que significa ser un hombre. De hecho, el titulo que Jesús se da a si mismo con mayor frecuencia es: "El Hijo del Hombre", que en su traducción original es el Hijo de Adán, es decir el Hijo del Humano, o a final de cuentas: El Humano- El Hombre.

Rohr habla de los cuarenta días en el desierto donde Jesús venció las tentaciones del Enemigo, como parte de la iniciación de

Jesús. El permaneció solo en el desierto y en silencio descubriendo su identidad. Y Jesús descubre ahí en medio de la lucha y de ser "ministrado por ángeles y bestias" que él es el Hijo Amado del Padre. Que el es Hijo, y que el es Amado, tal y como escuchó el día de su Bautismo. Por cierto, cabe decir que el Rito del Bautismo es originalmente un Rito de Iniciación. Es un rito donde uno muere y vuelve a nacer, por lo cual muchas de las pilas bautismales primitivas estaban hechas en forma de ataúd pues era un paso de muerte y de ahí un paso de resurrección y vida nueva. Toda iniciación esta basada en estos principios, de muerte y vida, de soledad y silencio, de lucha interna para así descubrir por uno mismo su propia identidad. Descubrir que uno es hijo, y que uno es un hijo amado del Padre. Hijo amado de Dios. Este descubrimiento transforma la vida.

Volviendo a San Pablo, vemos en su teología del Bautismo como esta claro que hay "morir con Jesús para renacer en El". Desgraciadamente el poder transformador del rito que se ha perdido pues hoy en día es más bien un rito/sacramento cultural, bonito, con vestido blanco, una ceremonia religiosa muchas veces no comprendida y que no transforma en lo concreto. Sabemos que en la teología católica el sacramento es eficaz aun en estos casos y aparece en germen la vida nueva. Pero si somos sinceros y vemos como en nuestros países latinoamericanos y cristianos millones de bautizados que no están transformados ni viven madura y responsablemente y mucho menos tienen una visión trascendental de la existencia. El bautismo no es "mágico" ni es un "seguro de vida" por si se llega a morir. Gracias a Dios ya no existe el fabricado concepto del "limbo" en la teología actual.

En el Nuevo Testamento vemos como San Pablo constantemente habla de la lucha entre "la carne y el espíritu". El no habla de la "carne" como el cuerpo o lo sexual como generalmente se piensa, el habla de "carne" como aquello que se opone al Espíritu de Jesús. Lo podríamos llamar "el ego" o "el falso yo" en términos de Tomas Merton. Es por eso que el "Ego" debe morir y ser sepultado con Cristo. El otro término Paulino es "el hombre viejo" que es crucificado y el "hombre nuevo" que renace por el Espíritu. Lo importante no son los términos sino la experiencia autentica de muerte y resurrección, de transformación por el descubrimiento de la verdadera identidad de uno mismo, Identidad de Hijo de Dios y amado por Dios. Fíjense como se parte desde el comienzo (iniciación) del amor y no del temor o la culpa como se ha predicado por siglos. Quizá la culpa y la obligación hacen a la persona ir a la iglesia o el templo, o llevan a muchos a rechazar por completo la religión, pero no llevan a la persona a una transformación espiritual y psicológica. Más bien, en mi experiencia pastoral y clínica, esa religión basada en el miedo y la culpa es fuente de mucha ansiedad y escrúpulos, y hoy en día, es fuente de cinismo o fanatismo. Nada tienen que ver con una verdadera y sana espiritualidad que le da sentido a la vida y cambia el corazón. Los ritos de iniciación tienen como objetivo llevar al joven a esa experiencia transformadora basada en la bondad de Dios y en su creación.

Ahora bien, en todas las culturas donde se perdieron los ritos de iniciación, existen "pseudos-iniciaciones" para los varones. Generalizando un poco, veamos algunos de estos pasos de iniciación donde existen algunos que ayudan en cierta forma al joven a madurar, pero muchas veces maduran en un área manteniendo otra área de su alma sin desarrollar. El estudio de los arquetipos masculinos ilumina nuestra comprensión del alma del varón.

Existen jóvenes que se van al ejército y en su entrenamiento reciben alguna forma de iniciación. Usualmente esta iniciación es solo al arquetipo del guerrero y no a los demás arquetipos especialmente el sabio o el amante, mucho menos al arquetipo del Rey. También existen los "boys scouts" que son buenos para formar en algunas áreas al joven. En la vida religiosa existe el "noviciado" que es una forma intensa de iniciación para el muchacho con grandes ilusiones de servir al prójimo y a Dios. Sin embargo, puede haber un gran deseo espiritual pero algo desencarnado, rechazado por siglos de tabú, el cuerpo y los sentidos. Pero usualmente el concepto de llegar a ser hombre parte de otro lugar. Vemos como el concepto de ser hombre muchas veces parte de estereotipo cultural y a veces solo por observación de lo que acontece en la televisión, el cine, la sociedad, o la casa. Por ejemplo, en algunas culturas, el joven pasa a ser "hombre" cuando tiene su primera experiencia sexual. Claro que puede ser un momento transformante, pero usualmente es presionado, sin un contexto y peor aún, sin compromiso ni amor. Algunos papas llevan a sus hijos varones al prostíbulo para que "se vuelvan hombres". Para otros el ser "hombre" es el saber pelear y mostrar violentamente su masculinidad. Todos sabemos que también el beber en exceso es para muchos muestras de dejar de ser niño y ahora ser "hombre". Otro ejemplo que vemos en nuestras calles es el de las pandillas o bandas donde muchos muchachos tienen sus iniciaciones, y en algunas de estas bandas estas iniciaciones incluyen algún crimen serio inclusive el asesinato de alguien. En las universidades también hay semi-ritos de iniciación, pero no hay "ancianos sabios" que guíen al joven en estos procesos que usualmente son solo maneras muy infantiles de avergonzarse a sí mismos o a sus compañeros de fraternidad.

Pasos de la Iniciación

En una manera sencilla de explicar el proceso de maduración e iniciación del varón, se puede decir que en la vida existen dos etapas. La primera etapa es la "subida", el ascenso. Es donde el varón aprende disciplina, valores, religión, responsabilidad. El hombre comienza a luchar y muchas veces a triunfar en la vida, en los deportes, en el trabajo, en la conquista de su prometida. Para muchos hombres, toda la vida se trata de esto. Una visión blanca y negra de la realidad, de quienes están bien y quienes están mal, de los buenos y los malos. Esta etapa sigue siendo una etapa inmadura, pues el varón usualmente culpará a alguien cuando las cosas no le salen como el quiere. El hombre se siente muy a gusto en su "torre de control" localizada en la cabeza. Vive ahí y difícilmente desciende al corazón y a sus entrañas. Desde de un punto de vista religioso, en esta primera etapa el varón conoce su catecismo. Puede también conocer textos bíblicos y asistir a grupos de oración. El esta sumamente involucrado en su iglesia y en cuidar su religión. Naturalmente el quiere ser "ortodoxo" y seguir las reglas y lineamentos de su religión al pie de la letra. Se molesta con los que difieren y de alguna forma mantiene una actitud de superioridad pues para el su forma de ver y vivir su religión es la correcta. Es claro que esta etapa es necesaria para los niños y para los adolescentes. Ellos necesitan claridad y necesitan conocer los límites, acatarse a las reglas, y conocer las leyes. Pero cuando un varón es físicamente mayor y se mantiene en esa dimensión linear y meramente conceptual de la religión, su espiritualidad queda coartada.

En la Iglesia Católica existe el Ministerio de la Palabra. Este ministerio corresponde a la dimensión profética de la misión de Cristo. El ministerio de la palabra es un proceso dinámico en etapas que comienza con el Primer Anuncio o Kerigma que es parte nuclear de la Evangelización. Desgraciadamente este primer anuncio es, en palabras del P. Alfonso Navarro MsSp, la laguna más grande de la Iglesia Católica. Sin entrar en detalles, el objetivo del Primer Anuncio es llevar a los destinatarios a una experiencia del Dios vivo, de encuentro con la persona de Jesús.

El segundo momento del ministerio de la Palabra es la catequesis. La catequesis equivale al discipulado, es el momento de la formación doctrinal que lleva a la unidad de la fe y al conocimiento mas íntimo de la persona de Jesús. Parece ser que muchas de las energías de la Iglesia están centradas en este elemento, pero por lo general esta etapa se enfoca únicamente en los niños y es solo una preparación sacramental. También parecería ser que para los adultos el énfasis continua siendo el saber lo que el Catecismo dice y creer conceptualmente en las afirmaciones que el Catecismo presenta. Sin disminuir la importancia que tiene este elemento, muchas veces es hasta aquí donde llega la formación de millones de varones (y mujeres) en el mundo. Algunos privilegiados llegan al tercer momento del ministerio de la palabra, la teología. Pero como sabemos bien, son muy pocos los que están formados a este nivel.

Menciono estos principios pues es importante que quede claro que la iniciación de los varones y la espiritualidad masculina de la que se esta hablando en este artículo, incluye y valora las etapas del ministerio de la palabra. Pero volviendo a las etapas del desarrollo de la vida del varón, la evangelización y la catequesis ayudan solo en la primera etapa, la etapa de ascensión. Ahora bien, es sumamente necesaria la siguiente etapa del descenso para llegar a una mayor profundidad en la espiritualidad. La iniciación de los varones pretende ayudar a los hombres a "bajar" y a llegar a una dimensión no dualista de la realidad. Es necesario recuperar ritos de iniciación para varones que nos ayuden a profundizar en nuestra fe, en el camino de la espiritualidad, a madurar emocional y psicológicamente para así llegar a obtener algo de sabiduría para poder guiar a las generaciones siguientes de muchachos buscando dirección.

La adaptación de ciertos ritos de iniciación para la cultura occidental mantiene los mismos principios y pasos que los ritos originales de iniciación. Revisemos cuales son estos pasos de la iniciación. El primer paso es sacar de su ambiente conocido y confortable al varón. Es decir, hay que llevar al varón fuera de lo que es cómodo para el. Este lugar de lo que hablamos es un lugar físico, psicológico, y espiritual. Físicamente todos los ritos de iniciación ocurren en la naturaleza y no en salones de clase. Muchos varones respetan y admiran la naturaleza y ven en ella algo trascendente que no se puede controlar. Psicológica y espiritualmente el varón tiene que estar en un espacio "liminal". Este es un espacio sagrado y no profano. Literalmente la palabra liminal significa algo semejante a "el lugar entre el medio". Es como haber salido de un cuarto sin haber entrado en el siguiente. En términos del béisbol, seria como estar entre bases, por ejemplo, haber salido de la primera base y aún no haber llegado a estar "safe" en segunda. Está uno en medio.

En términos laborales podría ser el estado anímico de alguien que ha perdido su trabajo pero tiene una entrevista prometedora en una nueva compañía. Relacionalmente es el lugar de paso entre una relación y otra, o la pena experimentada al perder a alguien amado.

Una vez que el varón es llevado a la naturaleza, se le pide que el sea un participante activo y no un espectador del evento. Es necesario tener la mente de principiante ("beginner's mind"), o en términos cristianos: ser como niño. En la naturaleza se les invitará al silencio para así poder escuchar la voz de Dios y descubrir su llamado e identidad. Así que este primer paso es un paso de separación- separar al hombre de si mismo, de su lugar cómodo, de su identidad falsa formada por años de mensajes culturales estereotipados.

Cuando el varón o la mujer pierden algo de su identidad falsa (ego) o pierde algo de su vida que ama y aprecia, la experiencia es una de dolor. Desgraciadamente al varón no se le ha permitido sentir y expresar su pena. Lo que el hombre comúnmente hace es guardarse esos sentimientos que trágicamente luego se manifiestan en diversas disfunciones adictivas. Es también muy común que el hombre exprese mucho enojo y agresión cuando realmente lo que siente es un profundo dolor interno. Sabemos como se le es permitido al varón el expresar su enojo pero no se le permite tradicionalmente llorar. Si comprendemos esta dinámica psicológica entenderemos porque hay tanta violencia y agresión en la familia, la sociedad, y el mundo. El segundo paso de la iniciación es por lo tanto, el momento del duelo. El sentir y llorar si acaso es necesario, todas las pérdidas de la vida. Perdidas físicas de salud y vitalidad, perdidas emocionales de relaciones pasadas y traiciones experimentadas, perdidas terribles de inocencia o de muertes familiares, etc. La perdida final y radical es la muerte del ego. Ese ego que el varón ha construido por muchos años y defiende día a día con argumentos y posturas de poder y control. "El que quiera seguirme, que se niegue a si mismo, tome su cruz, y sígame". Para los budistas este desprendimiento del ego es la clave de la iluminación y el apego al ego es la fuente de todo sufrimiento. Esta etapa de duelo se conoce en la psicología como "grief work", es decir, "trabajo de duelo". Y créanme, este es un trabajo arduo y doloroso, pero bajo el prisma de la iniciación, uno lo vive junto a otros varones, bajo la guía de sabios ancianos, y bajo la mirada amorosa de Dios.

Cuando se quita de en medio al falso yo, entonces uno esta abierto a descubrir el autentico yo, creado a imagen y semejanza de Dios. Es necesario por lo tanto tener un tiempo largo de soledad, ayuno, y silencio para ahí descubrir nuestra identidad. Recordemos los 40 días de desierto en la vida de Jesús. Para los nativos americanos, la iniciación incluye el envió del joven solo, en la búsqueda de su nombre y su visión ("vision quest"). ¿Quien soy? ¿Cual es el propósito de mi vida? ¿Dónde estoy y a dónde voy?

En esa búsqueda se les dan a los varones unos mensajes de iniciación. El varón esta ya dispuesto, despojado de su hombre viejo, buscando respuestas. Puede entonces escuchar mensajes de sabiduría tales como: "tu no eres el centro del mundo", "no tienes control sobre todo" y otros mensajes que prefiero guardar por ahora en silencio.

Es en el silencio, en la aparente soledad, y en la naturaleza donde Dios se puede escuchar y ver. La oración contemplativa es por lo tanto algo esencial de la iniciación. Uno aprende a ver con ojos nuevos y a escuchar lo que el viento dice. Toda espiritualidad esta basada en la capacidad de ver lo que realmente es. Es un contacto con lo real. Es el encuentro con el Dios Vivo presente en el presente. Al ver y oír uno descubre su vocación e identidad. Uno descubre que es "hijo amado" y que uno tiene a un "Padre" que lo ama incondicionalmente. El varón pierde el temor con el que ha vivido por tantos años, pues una vez que el ego muere ya no hay nada más que defender. Sabemos quienes somos y no hay porque más pretender. Es el momento de la iniciación.

Finalmente el varón regresa a la comunidad. Este regreso esta marcado por las señales del combate. Las heridas de la vida son ahora heridas sagradas. El joven ha entrado en la batalla y ha matado al dragón que le amenazaba. Y el varón no regresa a vivir independiente y solo, sino que regresa a la comunidad para servirla. El niño es ahora un hombre y viene a construir y defender su comunidad y su familia. El vuelve para ahora poder ser no solo hijo, sino también padre, padrino, tío, abuelo, y maestro de la generación siguiente. Este varón iniciado ya no establece sus relaciones con otros hombres basándose en la competencia y el poder. Ahora el puede cooperar con los demás hombres pues son sus hermanos y puede servir a la mujer que es ahora realmente su compañera. Este varón tiene un respeto por el mundo natural. No piensa más en explotar la naturaleza para enriquecerse sino que se descubre como parte de algo mucho mayor que el: el planeta tierra. El ya no es el centro del universo, sino que ahora pertenece a un universo que lo trasciende infinitamente en tiempo y espacio. Este hombre respeta toda forma viviente, el mundo material, las plantas, los animales y toda la creación.

La espiritualidad masculina es una espiritualidad de acción y contemplación. No esta basada en conceptos, palabras, y debates ideológicos. Esta espiritualidad es la que vemos en Juan el Bautista, Pablo y Pedro, Abraham y David, San Francisco y San Ignacio, Martín Luther King y Nelson Mándela por mencionar algunos. Es una espiritualidad no violenta como lo vemos en Gandhi. Es la espiritualidad de Jesús, el Hijo del Hombre, que no vino a ser servido sino a servir y que no quedo atrapado en las promesas ilusas del poder, placer, y parecer. Jesús de Nazaret fue un hombre libre. El encarno claramente los cuatro arquetipos masculinos del rey, el guerrero, el sabio, y el amante.

En mi experiencia pastoral y clínica me encuentro varones que están listos para dar otro paso más allá del materialismo capitalista y el cinismo existencial. Me encuentro con varones que han perdido a sus parejas por falta de afecto y comunicación. Me encuentro a niños y adultos con un hambre de padre, de un hombre adulto que los ame y los guíe. Hombres que están inconformes con mucha de la ideología y estructura institucional de la religión. Sabemos como las mujeres intuyen la falta de maduración del hombre. Muchas veces son las mujeres las que impulsan al varón a ser iniciados y a buscar una espiritualidad. Pienso que este descubrimiento y esta área que comienza a estudiarse sobre la espiritualidad masculina es clave para bienestar del varón, de la familia, de la sociedad, y del planeta. Yo les invito a reflexionar sobre la posibilidad de una sociedad formada por varones adultos que han sido iniciados y han renacido por el agua, el fuego, y el Espíritu. La espiritualidad masculina es jornada y una aventura que vale la pena vivir.

Bibliografía

Bly, Robert. (1992). *Iron John- A Book about Men*; First Vantage Books Edition.

Frankl, Victor. (2002).*Man's Search for Ultimate Meaning*; New York, NY.

Grun, Anselm. (2006). *Luchar y Amar*; Buenos Aires, San Pablo.

Hollis, James. (1994). *Under Saturn's Shadow- The Wounding and Healing of Men*; Inner City Books, Canada.

Kelly, E.W.; (1990). *Spirituality and Religion in Counseling and Psychotherapy*; Alexandria, VA. American Counseling Association

Maslow, A. H. (1974). *Religions, Values, and Peak-Experiences*; Penguins Books.

May, Gerald G., M.D. (1988). *Addiction and Grace*; San Francisco: Harper & Row.

Moore, Gillette. (1991). *King Warrior, Magician, and Lover- rediscovering the archetypes of the mature masculine*; Harper, San Francisco, CA.

James, William; (1963) *The Varieties of Religious Experience: a study in human nature*; New Hyde Park, NY.

Ramirez, Antonio. (2002). *The relationship between Spiritual Well-Being and Psychological Well-Being among Mexican-American Catholics*; St. Mary's University, TX, (dissertation).

Johnson, A. Robert. (1989). *He: Understanding Masculine Psychology*; Harper Row, New York.

Rohr, Richard, (1994). *Quest for the Grail.* Crossroad Publishing Company; New York, NY.

Rohr, Richard & Martos, Joseph. (2006). *De Hombre Salvaje a Hombre Sabio-Reflexiones sobre espiritualidad masculina*; Buena Prensa, A.C., México.

Rohr, Richard. (2004) *Adam's Return: the five promises of male initiation*; New York: Crossroads Pub.

Rohr, Richard (2004). *Soul Brothers- men in the Bible speak to men today*; Maryknoll, NY. Orbis Books.

Rolheiser, Ronald. (2003). *En Busca de Espiritualidad-lineamientos para una espiritualidad cristiana del siglo XXI*; Ed. Lumen, Buenos Aires, Argentina.

Tolle, Eckhart, (2004). *The Power of Now: a guide to spiritual enlightenment*; Vancouver, B.C., Canada.

The Jewish Setting of the Lord's Prayer
Peter E. Roussakis

Churches across the globe pray the Lord's Prayer in their weekly worship services. One of the aspects of the prayer of which most Christians are unaware, or at least have not taken the time to think about, is the setting within which the prayer arose. This brief essay highlights the Jewish matrix from which the Lord's Prayer was spawned.[1]

Intention

The most obvious matter to note first regarding the Jewish setting of the prayer is that which we observe from the Lukan account. "One day Jesus was praying in a certain place. When he finished, one of his disciples said to him, 'Lord, teach us to pray just as John taught his disciples'" (Lk. 11:1). As Barclay commented, "It was the regular custom for a Rabbi to teach his disciples a simple prayer which they might habitually use. John had done that for his disciples, and now Jesus' disciples came asking him to do the same for them."[2] The custom in Jesus' day for a Rabbi to teach his followers a prayer which was specifically of his composition and would be uniquely theirs to pray was a *mark of identity* with that particular Rabbi. This *intention* is the most conspicuous evidence of the Jewish setting of the prayer.

Content

Secondly, the *content* of the prayer is indicative of Old Testament Jewish thought. Without elaboration, a few examples of content parallels God as Father (Isa. 63:16, Ps. 89:26), God's Name (Ex. 20:7, 2 Sam. 6:2, Jer. 7:10-11), the doing of God's will (Ps. 119:30-33), God's provision for daily bread (Ex. 16:14-21), God's forgiveness (Ps. 130:4, and throughout the Old Testament), God's protection (Ps. 91:14, Pr. 2:8), God's deliverance (1 Sam. 12:10, Ps. 3:8, Ps. 32:7), and God's praise (1 Chr. 29:10-13, Dan. 2:20, the Psalms). Because of the ideational connection of the Lord's Prayer with Old Testament thought, Kenneth Stevenson has referred to the Lord's Prayer as a "canonical prayer."[3]

Shape and Direction

A further correspondence with Jewish piety is the *shape* of the Lord's Prayer echoed in other Old Testament inclusions. The *Shema* (Deut. 6:4-5) served the Jews as a confession of faith.[4] "Its threefold sequence of heart, soul and strength could have inspired the 'twice threefold' arrangement of [Jesus'] own prayer given to the disciples."[5] Most certainly Jesus, as all Jews, would have recited/prayed the *Shema* twice daily.[6]

The twofold *direction* of the Lord's Prayer with the first three petitions being directed God-ward, and the second group of three focusing on human concerns, is similar to that of the Ten Commandments; the first four Commandments speaking of respect and duty to God, while the remaining six emphasize regard and duty to others. It is worth noting this two-part direction and movement is seen as well in the Beatitudes (Mt. 5:3-12). In content, shape, and direction of thought, the Lord's Prayer echoes the Jewish piety of the Old Testament era, piety which was also a part of Jewish life in Jesus' day.

Prayer Tradition

Another major area with which the Lord's Prayer has similarities is the Jewish prayer tradition of the synagogue. A quote from G. Campbell Morgan will serve to introduce this.

> It has been affirmed and correctly so that [the Lord's Prayer] is not a new prayer. Its every petition is to be found in the Talmudic writings… There can be little doubt… that the men who heard the Master, when He first gave them the prayer, were familiar with all its petitions. In all probability they had used them constantly in their worship from childhood… [Jesus] gathers together the things with which they were most familiar and placed them in such perfect relation to each other as to reveal as never before the whole plane of prayer.[7]

Two things upon which we shall comment from Morgan's quote are the "Talmudic writings" and "their worship".

The *Talmud* was written between the third and sixth centuries CE. Its significance is that it is the written record of accumulated Jewish oral tradition of theological import as far back as 450 BCE. After many hundreds of years of oral transmission, the teachings of Rabbis were put into print. We in the Christian tradition might think of the Talmud (meaning study or learning) as a commentary on and application of the Torah (law/instruction), the first five books of the Old Testament. In the Talmud all aspects of Jewish life are discussed.[8] In it there is a record of Jewish liturgical memory, and it is this material which has particular bearing on the present consideration of the Lord's Prayer's Jewish setting. As we shall see, what Jesus offered may very well have been a condensed version of other Jewish prayers which he and his disciples and all other devout Jews would have prayed publicly in the Temple and synagogue as well as in private devotions. There would have been a familiarity with the phrases of the Lord's Prayer. The disciples would have grasped the significance of them, and they would have been easily remembered.

Moreover, it is also known from the Talmud that "it was customary for prominent masters to recite brief prayers of their own in addition to the regular prayers of worship; and there is indeed a certain similarity noticeable between these prayers and that of Jesus."[9] What were some of the Jewish prayers upon which the above statements have their basis?

Two prayers included in synagogue worship with which the Lord's Prayer possesses parallel aspects are the *Kaddish* and the *Amidah*.[10] According to Kenneth Stevenson, the Kaddish, which is Aramaic for "holy" referring to the praise of God, has occurred in various versions. For example, appearing in a prayer book, *Seder Tefillot*, compiled in the ninth century CE, the text of the Kaddish reads (with similarities to the Lord's Prayer in italics added):

Exalted and sanctified be His great Name.

In the world which He created *according to His will*, may *He establish His kingdom*

in your lifetime, and in the lifetime of the entire House of Israel, speedily and soon.

May *His great Name be blessed for ever and to all eternity.*

Praised, glorified, exalted, extolled, revered, highly honored and adored is the Name

of the Holy One, blessed be He beyond all the blessings, hymns, praises and consolations that are ever uttered in the world.[11]

Settings of the Kaddish longer than this example were used by the synagogue preacher at the close of his exposition of scripture and at eulogies for the deceased. A Kaddish may also be used by the congregation in response to the synagogue preacher's sermon. Shorter versions were used by devout Jews in their daily private prayers[12] as in the following (italics added):

> *Exalted and hallowed be His great Name* in the world which He created *according to His will. May He establish His kingdom* in your days, and in the lifetime of the whole household of Israel, speedily and at a near time. Amen.[13]

Baruch Graubard describes the Kaddish as "one of the most frequently repeated prayers in the traditional synagogue service… That prayer is the doxology *par excellence* of the synagogue liturgy…"[14]

The second Jewish prayer with which the Lord's Prayer has parallels is commonly referred to as the *Amidah* (standing) because of the posture of the worshipers when it is prayed. The Amidah is more specifically called the Eighteen Benedictions *(Shemone Esre Berakoth),* which were a part of the daily synagogue service. The Hebrew word translated *benedictions* is *berakoth*. It may also be rendered *eulogies* or *blessings*. In Jewish liturgy a benediction is a prayer which begins or ends with "You are praised, O Lord", "Blessed be Thou, O Lord", or "Blessed are You…". The Amidah and the "Shema and Its Blessings"[15] together serve as two central units of the synagogue service.[16] Every devout Jew is expected to pray these prayers in their daily private prayers as well.

In the Talmud the sacred memories of the origins of the Amidah going back to the prophets are included.[17] The first three of the blessings of the Amidah are expressions of praise. The greater number, four through fifteen, are petitions, which explains why the Amidah is additionally referred to as *Tefillah* (The Prayer).[18] Tefillah is petitionary prayer, the basic Jewish form of prayer.[19] The last three benedictions are again expressions of praise and thanksgiving.

The following are examples from the Amidah which are paralleled in the Lord's Prayer.[20]

Our Father is present in benedictions five and six. Benediction six begins:

> Let us return, our Father, unto Your Torah.

Hallowed be thy Name is echoed in the third benediction.

> Holy are You and holy is Your Name;
> and holy ones praise You everyday.
> You are praised, O Lord, the holy God.

The themes of *Thy kingdom come, thy will be done* are found in benedictions eleven through fourteen. The fourteenth includes:

> Return in mercy to Jerusalem, Your city.
> Dwell in it, as You have promised.
> Rebuild it soon in our days as an
> everlasting building; and speedily
> set up in it the throne of David.
> You are praised, O Lord, Builder of Jerusalem.

The provision for *bread* is heard in benediction nine.

> Bless this year for us, O Lord our God,
> and all the varieties of its produce for good.
> Grant blessings upon the face of the earth,
> and satiate us out of Your goodness.
> Bless our year like the good years.
> You are praised, O Lord, who blesses the years.

Benediction thirteen speaks of the security of God's people as in the *lead us* and *deliver us* requests of the sixth petition of the Lord's Prayer.

Grant a good reward to all who trust in your Name,
and set our portion among them.
Then shall we never be ashamed,
for we trust in You.
You are praised, O Lord,
[Security] and Trust of the righteous.

And the closing doxology of the Lord's Prayer has similarities with the eighteenth benediction.

O our King, may Your Name be
praised and exalted continually
and forever and ever.

Conclusions

From all of the above, we may conclude that the Lord's Prayer is essentially Jewish in intention (mark of identity), content (ideational connection with Old Testament thought), shape (twice three-fold arrangement), and direction of thought (two-fold). Parallels in content and style (brief and petitionary) are observed in the tradition of Jewish prayer. The Lord's Prayer may be said to be a miniature portrait of Jewish prayer. It is more brief as with the Half-Kaddish, and more thematically inclusive as with the Amidah. It is understandable, therefore, why Hughes Oliphant Old commented: "It may be that the Lord's Prayer, which Jesus taught his disciples, is a shortened version of the Amidah."[21]

As with the 'Shema and Its Benedictions' and the Amidah which were prayed daily in the synagogue service, so we in the Christian church traditionally have included the Lord's Prayer as an integral part of the prayers of the people in corporate worship in such locations as the people's conclusion to the Invocation, after the pastor's Prayer of Intercession (or Pastoral prayer in some traditions), at baptisms, and as a part of the observance of the Lord's Supper.

Again, as with the Jewish tradition of praying the Shema twice a day and the Amidah three times daily in private prayers, so do many Christians pray the Lord's Prayer daily, and even pattern their private prayers according to the order and content of it, as does this writer. Early on, as evidenced in *The Didache*, Christians were encouraged to pray the Lord's Prayer three times a day.[22] Because the Lord's Prayer is a compendium of Christian belief, we are on solid ground for calling it a "canonical prayer". Praying it in worship is one way parishioners, perhaps without realizing it, are confessing their faith. While the Lord's Prayer is not a formal creed, it functions in corporate worship in such a way as does the Shema in Jewish worship.

Additionally, whereas Jewish prayer has a *longing* and *anticipatory* aspect to it, so also the Lord's Prayer has been described as having an eschatological tone. *Thy kingdom come* in Matthew's gospel especially falls within the context of Jesus speaking at length about the kingdom. There is no doubt the Lord's Prayer has an urgent eschatological tone and intent. However, to limit our interpretation to that aspect is a mistake. *On earth as it is in heaven*, *daily bread*, and *lead us not into temptation* are very now-oriented. We must be reminded that our Lord spoke often with double meaning language, as the Gospel of John's content so thoroughly illustrates. For example, on many occasions Jesus spoke of the heavenly in terms of the earthly. With respect to the *kingdom* in particular, he made it clear that it is not only a *future realm* (e.g. Mt. 13:36-43, Lk. 13:28-29), but also a *present reality* (e.g. Mt. 12:28, Lk. 17:20-21).

Jewish prayer, as evidenced above, not only has future longing elements, but also present concerns. Praying the Lord's Prayer regularly in public and private worship is a way for the people of God to express their dependency upon God for all things, both for now and for later; but especially for the present.

Finally, as mentioned above, compared with many Jewish prayers, the Lord's Prayer is brief. And yet, as with the Half-

Kaddish and the practice of Rabbis teaching their disciples a brief prayer which would be uniquely theirs and would serve as a mark of identity with that Rabbi, we realize the Lord's Prayer most certainly demonstrates that it is a Jewish prayer. More than that, however, with respect to its brevity, to this writer it seems that Jesus would have had in mind non-Jews who would become his followers as well. Not being familiar with Jewish prayer tradition, it would have been inappropriate to offer a prayer with more extended Jewish nuances, characteristics and content totally foreign to Gentiles. Jesus was not interested in non-Jews becoming Jews, as Peter and Paul realized and the Jerusalem Council would eventually conclude (Acts 10:34-35, 15:1-29). He wanted them to be Godly, God-worshipers, kingdom people possessing kingdom traits and dispositions, as with those given in the Beatitudes (Mt. 5:3-12). The Lord's Prayer's length makes it possible for all Christians, whether they are Gentiles or Completed Jews, to be identified with our Lord and united with one another. Community is certainly an important aspect of life generally, of Jewish history and life, of our Lord and the early church. Praying the *Lord's* Prayer in public worship is one of the ways we foster the unity of our spirits, and bind our hearts in Christian love.

Notes

1 This essay is largely chapter three of the author's *United in Prayer: Understanding and Praying the Lord's Prayer* (Meetinghouse Press, 2007), 15-24.

2 William Barclay. *The Gospel of Luke*, rev. ed. (Philadelphia: The Westminster Press, 1975), 143.

3 Kenneth Stevenson. *Abba Father: Understanding and Using the Lord's Prayer* (Harrisburg, Penn: Morehouse Publishing, 2000), 12.

4 Emil Schurer, *A History of the Jewish People in the Time of Jesus Christ* Second Division, Vol. III (Peabody, Mass: Hendrikson Publishers, Inc., 1995 edition), 84; and Jakob J. Petuchowski, "The Liturgy of the Synagogue," *The Lord's Prayer and Jewish Liturgy*, Jakob J. Petuchowski

and Michael Brocke, eds. (New York: The Seabury Press, 1978), 49-50.

5   Stevenson, *Abba Father*, 36.

6   Schurer, 84, and Petuchowski, "The Liturgy of the Synagogue," 48-50. In the morning the *Shema* was recited preceded by two benedictions (Heb. *berakoth*) and followed by one benediction. These are 'blessing' prayers, as in "Blessed are You, O Lord…". The *Shema* was also recited in the evening preceded by two benedictions and followed by two more. Because the Shema does not stand alone in these ways, it is appropriate to say the *Shema* is *prayed*. While Jewish liturgy has no creed as do Christians who recite the Apostles' or Nicene creeds or other statements of faith, the 'Shema and Its Blessings' functions in that role in synagogue worship.

7   G. Campbell Morgan. *The Practice of Prayer* (Belfast, Northern Ireland: Ambassador Productions, Ltd, 1995), 59.

8   The Talmud (study/learning), which overall is a commentary on Torah (law/instruction), has two parts. The first is the Mishnah (repeated study) which is the written record of many centuries of oral commentary on the law. Such oral commentary was memorized by repetition (repeated study). It is a systematized collection of the Oral Law of the Old Testament as well as the political and civil laws of Judaism, traced as far back as 450 BCE. The second part of the Talmud is the Gemara (completed study) which, after Mishnah was recorded, included written explanations and commentary on Mishnah. Gemara contains rabbinic discussions, explanations and amplifications of the content of Mishnah.

9   Kaufmann Kohler, "The Lord's Prayer." An internet-generated article from the Jewish Encyclopedia.com. The Talmudic parallels he cites are Tosef., Ber. iii. 7; Ber. 16b.-17a., 29b; Yer. Ber. iv. 7d.

10 One of the scholarly sources for understanding the Jewish setting of the Lord's Prayer and its parallels from Jewish prayer tradition is *The Lord's Prayer and Jewish Liturgy*, edited by Jakob Petuchowski and Michael Brocke. In this goldmine of material it is worth noting the contributions by Alfons Deissler, "The Spirit of the Lord's Prayer in the Faith and Worship of the Old Testament" (3-17); Jakob J. Petuchowski, "Jewish Prayer Texts of the Rabbinic Period" (21-43) and "The Liturgy of the Synagogue" (45-57); Baruch Graubard, "The Kaddish Prayer" (59-72); Simon Lauer, "Abhinu Malkenu: Our Father, Our King!" (73-79); Joseph Heinemann, "The Background of Jesus' Prayer in the Jewish Liturgical Tradition" (81-89); Gordon J. Bahr, "The Use of the Lord's Prayer in the Primitive Church" (149-155); Michael Brocke, "The Liturgies of Synagogue and Church. An Introduction" (205-220). Other sources of

information regarding the Jewish setting of the Lord's Prayer include *Elucidations III* of Cyprian; James H. Charlesworth, "Jewish Prayers in the Time of Jesus," *Princeton Seminary Bulletin* Supplement 2 (1992): 36-55; and Brad H. Young, *The Jewish Background to the Lord's Prayer* (Austin, TX: Center for Judaic-Christian Studies, 1984).

11 Kenneth W. Stevenson, *The Lord's Prayer: A Text in Tradition* (Minneapolis: Fortress Press, 2004), 26. The above example and the one to follow are referred to as "Half-Kaddish" because it is briefer than the longer "Full-Kaddish" which has additional expressions of praise.

12 Stevenson, *Abba Father*, 56-57.

13 Petuchowski, "Jewish Prayer Texts of the Rabbinic Period," 37.

14 Graubard, "The Kaddish Prayer," 59.

15 See note 6 above.

16 Petuchowski, "The Liturgy of the Synagogue," 55.

17 Rabbi Lawrence A. Hoffman, ed., *My People's Prayer Book: Traditional Prayers, Modern Commentaries* Volume 2, *The Amidah* (Woodstock, Vermont: Jewish Lights Publishing, 2003), 21.

18 Ibid., 11.

19 Alfons Deissler described the Lord's Prayer as 'biblical tefillah' in "The Spirit of the Lord's Prayer," 4.

20 The examples are from Jakob Petuchowski, "Jewish Prayer Texts from the Rabbinic Period," 30-34.

21 Hughes Oliphant Old. *Worship: That is Reformed According to Scripture* (Atlanta: John Knox Press, 1984), 94.

22 James A. Kleist, trans. "The Didache," in Ancient Christian Writers (New York: The Newman Press, 1948), 8.3 [p. 19].

Re-imagining the Anglican Communion
Vincent Strudwick

Preliminaries

Let's be clear; the Episcopal Church, the Church of England and the Anglican Communion *are* in crisis. It is a crisis so serious that the repercussions of the controversy that is raging in our Communion of nearly 70 million people world-wide will ripple out into civil society, and profoundly affect the lives of ordinary people in ways which we can only begin to sketch. On the surface, the disagreements are about homosexuality, and personal morality; but beneath the surface there is a divergence in passionately held opinion about issues of the Gospel in Public Life, the nature of 'Authority' and especially the authority of scripture, and the Church's relationship with other Faiths. In all these issues there is 'difference' about how the Church faithfully changes in the historical process.

Meanwhile, although the media report, and often *mis*report, the crisis with relish, many of those 70 million people have no idea that there *is* a crisis – especially in parts of Africa, Asia and indeed the United Kingdom.

These ordinary Christians are getting on with life, earning a living, caring for their children, attending Church and trying to live as disciples with only the vaguest ideas about 'the crisis' and its implications. However, in many ways, their 'belonging' to the international family of the Anglican Communion brings a sharing of resources that affect many of the things that are important to them. The disintegration of the Communion would be a tragedy.

As far as the Church of England is concerned, disagreements and tensions are part of its history. From time to time, issues of 'difference' have erupted into 'crisis', from which the Church has eventually emerged. It has to do with the kind of Church we are . I would dare to put it like this. 'The Church of England emerged from controversy and debate in the 16th century, not around one set of theological principles, but rather as a big tent that gathered the hopes and aspirations of the English as they created a Church within a society at the beginning of a new age.'

To illustrate one aspect of this 'big tent' from my own experience of nearly fifty years of ordained ministry in the Church, I have frequently been a teacher or preacher, not only in England but in different parts of the Communion. I have travelled in the USA (very frequently), in Canada, in the Republic of South Africa, in Losotho, in Ghana, and in different parts of the diocese of Europe.

On more occasions than I can count, I have had conversations in which the variety of opinion among matters of belief and morals amongst us has been evident. For example, after a sermon, people will take me aside and they say:

"Thank you for what you said, but you know, what *I* think is...", and then they tell me. In response on many occasions I might often have replied 'Ah, you are a Sabellian then? - an Arian ? ,(how interesting !) It could be any one of the heresies 'condemned' early in Christian history, and often is one of them.

What am to do ? Lecture them ? Refuse them Communion ? I have never done either of those things. I have entered into many *conversations* from that starting point, being most of all delighted they are *thinking*. Knowing a little of the history of doctrine and morals, I see this diversity and questioning as being a common feature in the Church of England's history; for while that curious body has its roots in its Catholic past, it was shaped in the conflicts and changes of the 16th and 17th centuries, and has continued its process of formation to the present day, with variants in the communion to which it gave birth.

Knowing this history has profoundly affected my understanding of the present 'crisis'.

In his book 'Why Study the Past ?' The Quest for the Historical Church' Rowan Williams writes in the introduction:

'*History is a set of stories we tell in order to understand better who we are and the world we're now in*'

Yes, and he goes on to say something else: '*The Church claims… it is established…by God's activity. The challenge is to trace the ways in which the Church has demonstrated its Divine origin.*'

In my experience, it demonstrates it less by its certainty and more by its attitude of patient humble search. As my first teacher, Herbert Kelly once said, 'You're never wholly wrong - except when you think you're wholly right !'

In this essay I wish to help better the understanding of what the Anglican Communion has been, and might become, in the world we're now in, and how we may in our tradition discern God's guidance in the decisions that are before us.

The Church of England in Formation

The Church of England did not come sailing down the Thames in 1534 fully formed, nor has it ever become 'fully formed' at any time since then. During the whole 'long Reformation' as it is called, we see a Church containing great diversity, occasionally putting down markers and guidelines, (the 39 articles of Religion, the Book of Common Prayer) but essentially during the reign of Elizabeth 1st, the task was attempting to gather everybody 'in'. Here was no Protestant Reformation where the break with Rome was greeted by relief and rejoicing, but rather a long period of heart-searching in which people of settled, changed and changing opinions, sought to try to understand what God was up to, and work with him in it. While for political reasons – the security of the monarchy and the realm -there were cruel and terrible happenings, the aim of the Church of England's evolving ecclesiology was to include everybody *in;* so much so that a disapproving puritan Divine complained that the Church of England was like an 'Inn to which all are welcome', pleading that it should become more like its Calvinist cousins on the Continent with a better defined confessional position based on Scripture.

The person who in fact did most to articulate what the Church of England, indeed some would say he authored rather than articulated, was Richard Hooker, born in 1554 in Exeter and later a student then Fellow and Deputy Professor of Hebrew at Corpus Christi College Oxford.

Hooker's patron was Bishop Jewel, the author of the first little book to try to justify the Church of England published in 1562 entitled 'An Apologie of the Church of England.'

Hooker left Corpus and spent part of a year as a parish priest in Buckinghamshire (Drayton Beauchamp) before being whisked off to be Master of the Temple Church in London, a sort of Chaplain to lawyers in training. Here he engaged in the discernment process concerning the Church, in controversy and debate – particularly with Travers, his relative and deputy Master, who had Puritan leanings. It was reported: 'In the forenoon spake Canterbury, (Hooker) and the afternoon, Geneva' (Travers)[1]. Already a divide is seen between Reformation theology and the Church of England. In 1593 Hooker published the first three volumes of his eight volume work 'Of the Laws of Ecclesiastical Polity.' Now in our Church we do not have 'authorities' who speak for us all. But in Hooker we do have someone who was immensely influential in the continuing formation of our understanding of 'Church' and a conversation with him, in his context, is, I suggest, worthwhile, for from very early in the next century, it was to Hooker that people turned to understand the nature of the English Church.

What was Hooker's approach ?

Firstly, Hooker is a 'two book' man, believing that God speaks through the Creation as well as through Revelation. Therefore for Hooker, all people are graced by their birth, and he has a positive view of creation and of human beings' place in it. Of course, like all the Divines of the sixteenth century he takes seriously 'The Fall', but his language is very different to that of Calvin. Whereas Calvin describes the human condition after the Fall like this: 'famelicus saepe, saepe sitiens, semper miser', Hooker talks of the 'foggy damp' of Original Sin, blinding our vision and dampening our response, but happily leaving us still open to respond to the call to be fully human within the mystery of God's Providence. We may *all* be part of the mystical fellowship, for this membership, he says, is 'known only to God.'

So as far as the divisions in the Church are concerned, Hooker says we are 'divided into a number of distinct societies, every one of which is termed a 'Church' in itself' – but the world-wide Church on earth is one in its membership of the Mystical Body.

In this manner he embraces Roman Catholics during this time of religious separation. He says that we may not agree concerning 'her gross and grievous abominations' yet (and this is amazing for these times) 'touching those main parts of Christian truth wherein they constantly persist, we gladly acknowledge them to be of the family of Jesus Christ'. Note that – 'the family of Jesus Christ.'

Hooker seems aware that the politics and culture of the known world was changing, and poses the question: 'How can we embrace the *right kind of change*, and on what authority ?'

He challenges the view that a straight following of Biblical precedent is a sufficient way to run life in Society or in the Church.

'The sufficiency and perfection of Scripture', he argues, 'is a matter of the perfect capacity to do what it is *meant* to do' – and that is not to provide a template for everyday living in every generation. Rather, in what Hooker calls ' the change of times', we come to a view of how to understand and exercise our discipleship by reference to Scripture, enlightened by how others have interpreted it 'in the tradition'; that is to say, in '*their* historical circumstance, and 'guided by the light of natural understanding, wit and Reason.'

In making a judgement on this basis, Hooker acknowledges that we do not always get certainty. But this does not mean inaction. We must take the course 'where greatest probability lieth'.

Here is a fundamental theological principle, and it lies at the heart of how we in the Church of England, have approached change as part of the unfolding of the life process in history, through which God's purpose is fulfilled.

Hooker gives an example of how the ' Scripture as template' view may be challenged in describing the 'kiss of peace' issue. He suggests that in Scripture it is clear that in Christian gatherings of the early Church, such a kiss was exchanged. Today, he says, this is impossible. It would offend good manners, taste and propriety. So it should not be practised.

In 21st-century culture, of course, it is quite acceptable and the kiss of peace becomes almost an orgy in some Churches !

But this may be regarded as 'adiaphora' - a matter not at the heart of Christian teaching and morals. What about those things of great importance where difference is experienced ? Here Hooker acknowledges that we must be careful not to change 'because of the looseness and slackness of men' – that is to say, because we are caught up in a slide of *unprincipled* cultural change. Surely because of this danger we must stick to precedent and the clear word of Scripture?

While he seems clear that precepts of Scripture in matters of substance are ordinarily to be obeyed, he has a caveat to this. 'God never ordained anything that could be bettered', he writes, but 'new grown occasions' may cause what was once right to be regarded as outdated. We may not change God's ordinance, but we may recognise that He has changed it.[2]

Under the guidance of the Holy Spirit we are called into discernment; and Hooker recognises that there may be disagreement about the nature of what is discerned. Does this mean excluding and drawing tight boundaries ?

I don't think so. He writes: 'A more dutiful and religious way for us were to admire the wisdom of God which shineth in the beautiful variety of all things, but most in the manifold and harmonious dissimilitude of those ways whereby the Church on earth is guided from age to age through all the generations of men'.[3]

'*Eudiaphora*' is a word I have coined to describe matters of 'good'(sincerely held)difference, such as the issues of gender that face us today. But I confess, like many of my ideas, it hasn't caught on.

However the attitude it embodies has certainly been the 'motif' that has characterised the Church of England in its developing history, and held together a 'broad' Church which has enhanced the life of the nation.

Maurice Wiles, sometime Regius Professor at Christ Church, and Chair of the Church of England Doctrinal Commission wrote this:

> What is important for the Christian Community at large is not that it gets its beliefs absolutely clear and definite, it cannot hope to do that if they are really beliefs about God. It is rather that people within the community go on working at the intellectual problems, questioning, testing, developing and seeking the practical applications of the traditions that we have inherited from the past.

In other words, we may not always agree, but we are a learning Church as well as a teaching Church, and we need to stay together patiently seeking for the truth, the fullness of which belongs not to the Church, but to the Kingdom.

The 'Accidental' Communion

It would be difficult to argue that the Anglican Communion

came into being by 'intelligent design', although I do believe it has served the purposes of God in its history.

However, if ever there was an 'accidental communion' this is it. It was the outcome of British enterprise as people went to the New World 'for God and for Gain.' The spread of trading outposts, plantations and colonies ensured that the Cross followed the flag as trading ambitions were succeeded by Imperial dreams. America, India, and then in the 19th century Africa, Australasia and Asia saw the advent of Church of England missionaries, bringing with them the Book of Common Prayer, and eventually, Bishops, as England consolidated its Empire.

However, this Church of England outside England had no ecclesiology for that outlined by Hooker was not envisaged for anywhere but England. So in the Church of England overseas, outward conformity to Episcopal governance, together with the use of the Prayer Book, concealed a variety of understandings of the Scriptures and of doctrine, often dependent on the idiosyncracy of the individual missionary, or the flavour of the Missionary Society that sponsored him.

By the mid-19th century, Keble's attack on the perceived Erastianism of the Church of England, together with diverse responses to Darwin and the scientific challenge to the way Scripture had been interpreted, made the situation even more complex.

It was a missionary Bishop, John Colenso, the Bishop of Natal in South Africa, who set the cat among the pigeons. Colenso, had no problem accepting Darwin but he had taught Math at Harrow, and struggled with the arithmetic of Daniel and Ezekiel. Now, as he prepared to translate the Bible into Zulu, he addressed (for him) new and practical problems. As he had toured his new Diocese, he began to understand the relationship between polygamy and the economy, and although he did not approve of polygamy, he wished to deal sympathetically with converts, allowing them pastoral latitude and time. If a man has been converted at the age of 75 and has three wives, surely we don't have to break up the household ?

He also found he could not seriously expect his converts to believe the story of the Flood as historical event, and began to explore in what ways he could honestly consider the Bible to be 'The Word of God'.

His publications were soon in the public eye, but here was not an Oxford don ('Essays and Reviews' was in the making at home); here was a Missionary Bishop. Archbishop Grey of Capetown suspended him. Colenso responded that he was the Queen's bishop not Grey's and appealed to the Privy Council, to adjudicate for the Supreme Governor of the Church of England.

The issue of 'authority'- the authority of Scripture, and the authority for ministry, teaching and morals – had been raised in the fledgling 'Communion'.

The Canadian Church suggested the setting up of a Doctrine Commission which would draw up doctrinal regulations to which 'Anglicans' round the world should adhere. But this was very un-Church of England and was defeated. Instead it was agreed to call a ten yearly meeting of gentlemen Bishops at Lambeth, where they would agree guidance, and keep the ship afloat in a sort of Church of England way.

In fact it was not so silly as that image might suggest, and the Conference did bring some self understanding to the Communion, and provided a forum for ecumenical understanding as well. There were 76 Bishops at that first Conference, mainly Scottish, English and American by nationality, and many of them knew each other at Eton, Harrow or some other English school.

In 1888, the Conference of that year debated and affirmed the 'Chicago Quadrilateral'- a framework of four points that it was thought sufficient to hold the unity of this disparate Communion.

These were :

Adherence to Holy Scripture as containing all things necessary to Salvation, and as containing the 'rule and ultimate standard of faith'. However, the *interpretation* of Scripture was not considered.

Subscription to the Apostles and Nicene Creeds as being sufficient statements of faith,

The practice of Baptism and the Lord's Supper as being the two necessary Sacraments in the life of the Church, and

The presence of the 'Historic Episcopate' locally adapted to the needs of the various countries in which the Communion was present.

Over the years the Communion has grown.; by 1930, 300 Bishops attended and by 1988, after independence for most of the former Colonies, there were 800, reflecting a variety of cultures and languages, and theological traditions. 'Instruments of Unity' have been forged, with regular meetings of Primates together with a servicing bureaucracy in the Anglican Consultative Council.

As the so-called 'bonds of affection' in the Communion weakened under the pressure of political and cultural change, so the call for the formalisation of doctrine re-asserted itself.

In the Lambeth Conference of 1988, it was deemed necessary to set up a paper process whereby the Bishops would 'bring their Diocese' to Lambeth with them and following the Conference would 'take Lambeth back' to their respective dioceses. I was the Conference 'process consultant' for this exercise. Communication itself, let alone theological communication, was becoming more complex with the proceedings being translated into French and Spanish for non English speakers. This was a far cry even from Lambeth '68 when Archbishop Coggan had gathered everyone round the piano while he pounded out well known 'English' popular songs and choruses.

In '88, the call was for tighter structures. Should the coherence of Anglicanism be increased by strengthening the Centre, with a Papal-like Curia ?

Should there be another attempt to unify doctrine and pastoral practice ?

Interestingly, it was the official observer from the Reformed tradition at the conference, Elizabeth Templeton, who warned most cogently against this, when she called the Conference to think of doctrine as 'serious exploratory play – always some distance from the truth of God.'

Historically here was a fine Anglican attitude, being played back to us, as we were being tempted to abandon it.

It was indeed at Lambeth '98, ten years later, that the attack on historic Anglicanism was rejoined, and the seeds sown for the conflict in which, alas, we are now engaged.

The focus of the debate was on Homosexuality, and the passing of motion 1.10 assumed that the common basis of Scripture (to which reference was made) was the same as a common interpretation of Scripture, which takes us back not only to Hooker, but forward to explore the work of recent Biblical interpreters as we seek to understand what authority Scripture carries for us today.

This work is still before us; but what should have been an important debate within the Communion has been distracted by a series of events in which the consecration of Gene Robinson (a homosexual in a relationship) became the signal for breaking a number of conventions that had held the Communion together. The future of the Communion was put at risk with threats of expulsions, excommunications, and even refusals to be photographed together!

Many people asked: 'What does this mean for the collaborative work that goes on between Provinces of the Communion - for example, the digging of wells and the building of schools and Churches ? What does it mean in relation to friendships across borders and cross cultural theological exchange ? What message does it send to those estranged from Christianity, or those who have not yet heard the Gospel of love ?

Is there not something in Richard Hooker's 'Harmonious Dissimilitude' after all ?

Do we have to be dragooned into a coherence which has certainly never been our history as we move forward in a new century ?'

In 1993, Professor Sir Henry Chadwick, formerly Regius Professor of Divinity in the University of Oxford and Dean of Christ Church wrote:

> The Communion is a fairly loose federation of kindred spirits, often grateful for mutual fellowship, but with each Province preserving the right to make its own decisions.

There were many who believed that to re-assert this was the way forward, and a majority in the Episcopal Church took that view; but what has been described as 'the new Puritanism' was gathering force. The Churches where 'classical' Anglicanism had been nurtured – England itself, Australia, New Zealand, Canada – had suffered a variety of set backs as the wider population in those places became detached from their Anglican roots, with growing secularisation. In such places it has been the 'conservative' Churches that have grown. In Australia for example the very conservative 'new Puritan' Diocese of Sydney now comprises about one third of the entire Anglican church-going population of Australia.

Half the world's Anglicans are in Africa, and for complex reasons, including what has been described as 'the Colonial Reckoning', there is a strong moral conservative element among them. This movement is well described in Muriel Porter's book 'The New Puritanism', and she describes its challenge to the Anglican tradition in the words of Stephen Bates of the (English) newspaper, *The Guardian*.

'Homosexuality is the line in the sand for conservative evangelicals, because it is the issue they have chosen. It has not been thrust upon them – they spotted it as a rallying point more than decade ago. They see it as a way to unite their constituency in opposition to the shifting sands of belief and secular culture. For them, there is no room for dialogue, doubt or debate.' Theirs is nothing less than 'a take-over bid, to create a pure church of only one sort of believer.'[4] From being 'an Inn to which all are welcome', the Communion would be transformed to the bible based reformed sect for which the Puritans had hoped.

In my view, this should be resisted firmly, but in charity. The Covenant proposal seemed to be a way of doing this.

From Conflict to Covenant ?

The Windsor Report offered the idea of a Covenant in place of strife. The Churches of the Communion should covenant together to hold the unity while they worked at their disagreements. From the beginning though, it was clear that there were two ideas of what the Covenant should be.

Should it rest on one of the Biblical models of Covenant, where the common feature is the identification of a Promise from God, which requires a response from his people who covenant obedience to him ?

In this case, the Scriptural promise contained in the Gospel according to John, chapters 15 and 16, articulates an understanding of the Holy Spirit as enabling the created order to become what it was intended to be, and speaks of the Holy Spirit empowering the Church to engage in the search for truth and unity – an eschatological activity culminating in the Kingdom.

Such a proposed Covenant would remind us of the *unwritten* Covenant of this kind which has been fundamental in the life of the Church of England, and enabled us to live in Harmonious Dissimilitude for over four centuries.

Alternatively (as the new Puritans believe), the Covenant should be an opportunity at last to settle the questions raised in the sixteenth and early seventeenth centuries, and become the occasion to create a Communion with clear boundaries, an unequivocal basis in the authority of Scripture as the guide for life, and a more centralised, uniform administration with a (sound) Archbishop of Canterbury (or some other Primate) and a Curia at its centre.

Both ideas have been expressed as the Covenant idea has been debated and refined.

I was part of a small ACC drafting group that took the idea of the Covenant forward and presented it in the form of a proposal to the Primates for their consideration. This in turn gave rise to the 'Covenant Design Group' which reported in an impressive document – but one that in my view did not clarify which of the two ideas of covenant it was espousing. The final paragraphs raised the spectre of expulsions and hard-line codification in spite of the eirenical language in which the whole document was couched.

As a result of the consultation process on the draft version of the Covenant, a new version is now before the Communion which, while affirming that the Communion has no central authority to dictate with juridicial force the affairs of any Province, outlines a so-called 'disciplinary process' for Provinces that any other Province deems to have threatened the unity of the Communion. This so called 'St Andrews Draft' is still not the final form and is currently being debated.

For my own part, as I reflect on our history, I see the way forward only as an acknowledgement that the fullness of truth belongs to the *Kingdom*, and that this involves the Church in its life and worship in every generation engaging in the activity of searching the Scriptures and 'the tradition', and using the reason that is God's gift to us, with the intention of coming to a mind about those great matters that divide us. At the same time during this protracted debate, we have to respect the integrity and good faith of those whose search is currently leading them to differing understandings in both doctrine and ministry. Can we not stay 'in communion', understanding that, while our perceptions of 'truth' now differ, we are working towards the eschatological goal?

I have heard it said that if such a Covenant were to be agreed on such terms, the Communion would dissolve in being a mere federation – but if Henry Chadwick is right, isn't that what it has always been?

It is now clear though, that we can never go forward on the basis of 'what has been'. We need to re-imagine the Communion in the light of our experience, recognising that there is a sizeable group of Anglicans who cannot agree to the historical 'big tent' that has conditioned our past. However, for those of us who hold to this, might not both our history and our acknowledgement of difference today provide a good model for the world-wide Church? I foresee that world-wide Christianity will have to embrace an enormous degree of diversity and provisionality in the future, and that we shall come to acknowledge that this stems from its faithfulness to the Divine calling.

If this is so, then the model of Church offered by the Anglican Communion, not meticulously defined, but one with fuzzy boundaries, may well be prophetic.

The ACC Joint Standing Committee Report on the Covenant proposal (March 2006) contained the following paragraph, which was in tune with what I have been suggesting.

> It is part of the genius of Anglicanism that it has proved capable of embracing a wide rang of Christian emphases derived from many sources. Successive Lambeth Conferences have emphasised the role of cultural diversity, social change, and theological development, and have demonstrated that there is a proper place in our life for change and disagreement as well as for consistency and continuity.

I think that genius is being rebuked by those assured of a certain kind of Biblical certainty, and that there will inevitably be damage to our family life in the Communion which the embracing of 'the Covenant as response to the promises of God' sought to avoid.

Demonstrating our Divine Origin?

This section title, like the previous one, has a question mark, for we are 'in process' and it is not clear what the outcome will be.

What is God up to in our world at this time? What is our role as '*God's Associates*' — Hooker's phrase — discerning and enabling that purpose in the every day ?

The Worship of the Church, which includes the study and learning of the people of God as well as their prayer, their activity, as well as their contemplation, should be directed towards unlocking the mystery of God's activity in the world, whereas, alas, in all sorts of ways it seems to lock it up, safely within the institution and its rules and its self-concern.

I suspect we demonstrate our Divine Origin as a Church by engaging with wonder-ful curiosity in what is unfolding in our time. In a recent book entitled 'The Shield of Achilles'[5], Philip Bobbit, a former Director of Strategic Planning in the United States Security Council, who in his time has been a history Research Fellow at Nuffield College, has suggested we are witnessing the demise of the Nation State, and the birth of what he calls 'The Market State.' The globalisation of the market, the migration of peoples, the change in cultural and social patterns of life are all part of an enormous political and cultural mutation, which has a knock-on effect for religious institutions. The issues raised engage us theologically, for as Archbishop Rowan pointed out in a recent speech, there has come with the change to a global market an erosion of moral values. Those who run things, he said, reject the notion that Society needs core values – but without such core values, what is deemed 'good' for people will be largely determined by powerful interest groups – dominated by 'the Market'. There needs to be, he said, a return to a moral society in which the State recognises 'wider considerations than those of immediate profit and security.' I believe therefore that in a multi-faith world, we in the Church need to be able to engage with Government, with other institutions and agencies, and other religions, in order to speak of the 'moral society' and of what a common social ethic in our age might be, but – and here I return to the need for the Communion to hold together – we shall speak with a weak voice if in our own Church we are not modelling a fellowship in which the Grace of Our Lord Jesus Christ and the

Love of God and the fellowship of the Holy Spirit is not manifestly present . We shall speak with a weak voice if our understanding of 'moral' is limited to angry disagreements about the nature of sexual relationships.

I have argued elsewhere[6] for the need of an intensified interfaith dialogue, which may be the basis for greater understanding of our traditions in forging a faith-based social ethic, embraced by all faith communities, which is distinct from the morality of the market into which our societies are sliding.

As it is my conviction that we should engage in the gender debates within the Communion and beyond on the basis of our traditional theological standpoint of searching scripture, tradition, *and reason,* so, I believe it is imperative that we engage in serious inter-faith dialogue, not as an in-house religious exercise, but in order that we may learn to live together in harmony under the law, and that we may learn how to influence the making of law together with other faith communities.

In today's secular society, we are in danger of all decisions being made in the light of market forces with grave moral and ethical implications.

If we can learn how to debate and live with difference within the Communion, we may learn how to debate and live with difference with other faith partners in our Society; but at the same time, we shall also discern issues upon which we may agree and unite, for the common good.

I really do believe that the 'Harmonious Dissimilitude' of the Communion can work towards being a model for dialogue and fellowship on a wider scale.

As this article goes to press, a sizeable group of Bishops of the Communion are planning to meet together in Jerusalem – before the Lambeth Conference. While they deny that this is 'an alternative Lambeth' it is difficult to view it as anything other than that. How many Bishops will then come on to Lambeth is not yet determined. Archbishop Akinola (Nigeria) and Archbishop Jensen

(Sydney, Australia) have already made clear that they will not.

This, together with the fragmentation of traditional Provincial authority in the United States, with parishes seeking 'other' Episcopal leadership from Bishops overseas, the 'old' way of envisaging the Communion is clearly at an end.

Whatever happens to the Covenant, while a majority of Bishops may gather at Lambeth, the Anglican Communion needs to be 're-imagined' for the 21st century, taking account of the realities of the schisms that have already occurred.

What should be the attitude of those who embrace what I have tried to describe as the 'historic' Anglicanism of the Church of England and Anglican Communion ?

It is a Catholic Missionary who speaks:

> Historically, a single response to the Christian message has grown and thrived…What we are coming to see is that there must be many responses possible to the Christian message, which we have hitherto neither encouraged nor allowed. We have come to believe that any valid positive response to the Christian message could and should be recognised and accepted as Church. That is the Church that might have been, and might yet be.

The process towards such a Church might be forged in part through the experience of the 'Anglican Agony', so I shall end with the words of an Anglican Bishop – the evangelical John Taylor, a former General Secretary of the Church Missionary Society and later Bishop of Winchester.

He is speaking of the Ecumenical Movement of the 20th century – positively because it brought us closer together, but also saying that now, the debating of points, and the attempt to satisfy doctrinal 'purity' before allowing 'Communion' will no longer do. He writes:

> The realities of global Christianity are such…that all future

talk of mutual 'recognition' must mean, not validation, as if by some board of examiners, but the glad realisation that someone momentarily mistaken for a stranger, is actually a member of the family.[7]

In Anglicanism, from our history, I believe we have not a woolly loose flabby Church, but a dynamic model of Church, distinguished by its inclusiveness, which will still serve well the purposes of God, as we re-envision it, and reshape it, in the new world of the 21st century. Anglicans should play to their strengths for the sake of the whole Church of God. They should embrace change with boldness in the light of their theological tradition, but while doing so, remember that those who seek 'other order' and maybe withdraw from 'the Communion', are still 'family'; and the restoration of family harmony should never leave the agenda.

Notes

1   By Isaac Walton in the second half of the 17th century. Walton's essay on 'Hooker's life and death' is printed in the two volume edition of the 'Works of that Learned and Judicious Divine, Mr Richard Hooker' edited by John Keble and published in 1836. All the Hooker quotations in this essay are from 'Of the Laws of Ecclesiastical Polity' and are quoted from the text of this edition.

2   Laws iii x 5

3   Laws iii xi 9

4   *The New Puritanism – the Rise of Fundamentalism in the Anglican Church.* Muriel Porter 2006

5   The Shield of Achilles Philip Bobbitt: War, Peace & the Course of History 2002

6   *Winter Change to Spring* Vincent Strudwick 2007 published for the GTF

7   This quotation and the one from the Catholic missionary to the Masai,

Vincent Donovan, (immediately above) are taken from John Taylor's prophetic essay 'The Future of Christianity' in *The Oxford Illustrated History of Christianity* ed John McManners 1990

About the Contributors

Senad Agic is Shaykh Muhammad Nazim Adil al-Haqqani Professor of Islamic Studies. He was born in Bosnia and Herzegovina and is Head Imam of the Bosniaks in America. He holds a bachelor's degree and a master's equivalent in Arabic from the University of Sarajevo. Dr. Agic earned the Doctor of Ministry and Doctor of Philosophy in Islamic Studies from the Foundation and in 2004 received the Jalaluddin Rumi Prize in Islamic Studies. In 2006, he was awarded the Imam Malik Fellowship from the Foundation. His published works include Immigration and Assimilation: The Bosnian Muslim Experience in Chicago and A Centennial of Bosniaks in North America, both published in English and Bosnian. He has also published many articles in various journals on Islamic and other topics. In 1989, Dr. Agic was named Imam at the Islamic Cultural Center of Greater Chicago in Northbrook, Illinois, where he currently serves. He has been active in interfaith programs and interfaith dialogue associations, and has participated in discussions on peace and conflict with and among religions on National Public Radio, Voice of America, Radio Free Europe, Deutsche Welle, and other media outlets around the world. Dr. Agic's academic interests focus on traditional Islam which shuns extremism and religious animosity in favor of coexistence, cooperation, dialogue, and mutual understanding, appreciation and respect. He is married and is the father of two children.

Dennis J. Billy, C.Ss.R., is Karl Rahner Professor of Catholic Theology. He is an American Redemptorist of the Baltimore

Province. He hails from Staten Island, NY, and was educated there through high school in local Catholic schools. He holds an A.B. in English Literature from Dartmouth College (Hanover, NH), a Phil.Cert. from St. Alphonsus College (Suffield, CT), and M.R.E. and M.Div. degrees from Mt. St. Alphonsus Seminary (Esopus, NY). After his seminary training, Father Billy's religious order asked him to continue studies with a view toward teaching. He went on to earn a Th.D. in Church History from Harvard University, a M.A. in Medieval Studies from the University of Toronto, a M.M.R.Sc. in Moral Theology from the Katholieke Universiteit of Leuven in Belgium, an S.T.D. in Spirituality from The Pontifical University of St. Thomas (Angelicum, Rome), and a D.Min. in Spiritual Direction from the Foundation. Father Billy is Professor of the History of Moral Theology and Christian Spirituality at the Accademia Alfonsiana of The Pontifical Lateran University in Rome. He has authored numerous books and published many articles in a variety of scholarly and popular journals and is also very active in retreat work and in the ministry of spiritual direction.

Robin Gibbons is Fellow, Dean of Studies of Foundation House/Oxford, and Alexander Schmemann Professor of Eastern Christianity. He was professed as a Benedictine Monk at St. Michael's Abbey Farnborough in England in 1973 and ordained priest in 1979. It was there that he became introduced to the Eastern Church, especially the Byzantine Tradition. He is also an iconographer and one of his major works can be found in the Monastery of Christ in The Desert (Abiquiu, New Mexico). He later transferred to the Eastern Rite (Greek Catholic). Fr. Gibbons studied Theology at the University of Kent, doing his Masters in Theology and his Ph.D. in Liturgy at Heythrop College, University of London, later taking a Master of Studies (M.St.) degree in Reformation history at Cambridge (Trinity Hall). He is also a member of the Academy of Teaching and Learning, a Fellow of the College of Preceptors and a Fellow of the College of Preachers. He has specialized in three related areas, Liturgy, the Art and Architecture of the Christian Church, and Eastern Christianity, and has taught (and still teaches) in these areas in several universities: London, Surrey, Cambridge and Oxford) as well as seminaries and other academic institutions in the U.K. He acted as Monastic formator in two monastic communities in the United States. Fr. Gibbons has written many articles and been a contributor to several books, in 2006 publishing a small monograph on *The Eastern Church* and a major work on Christian space, *House of God: House of God's People*. At present he is engaged in writing a book on Liturgical formation. His present work is Director of Theology and Religious Study Programmes and Departmental Lecturer in the Oxford University Department for Continuing Education. He is also the Associate Director of the Oxford University Theology Summer School. Fr. Gibbons is a Senior Member of Kellogg College and also the Assistant Pastor for the Greek Catholic Melkite Church in London and Great Britain.

Ann V. Graber is Professor of Logotherapy/Existential Analysis. Dr. Graber grew up in Europe and was educated in Austria. As a young adult she emigrated to the United States where she earned the Diplomate credential from the Viktor Frankl Institute of Logotherapy and subsequently joined the Institute's international faculty. In that capacity she initiated the Distance Learning Outreach, which has attracted students from six continents during the past twelve years. Being bilingual, she assisted in the development of a comprehensive curriculum in Franklian psychology in the English language. Searching for greater spiritual understanding led her to study at the Graduate Theological Foundation where she earned a D.Min. in Pastoral Counseling and the Ph.D. in Pastoral Psychology. Her book, *Viktor Frankl's Logotherapy: Method of Choice in Ecumenical Pastoral Psychology*, is in its second edition and has been translated into a foreign language. She has been a frequent presenter at regional and international conferences. During the 16th World Congress on Viktor Frankl's Logotherapy, 2007, Dr. Graber was the recipient of the Presidential Award presented for visionary leadership, unselfish service, and distinguished contributions in promoting the work of Viktor E. Frankl throughout the world. At the Foundation, Dr. Graber serves as the contact person and liaison for students interested in pursuing the Diplomate credential from the Institute that is accepted by the Foundation toward three degrees: Doctor of Ministry (D.Min.), Doctor of Psychology (Psy.D.) and Doctor of Philosophy (Ph.D.), each with a specialization in Franklian Psychology.

C. Anthony Hunt is E. Franklin Frazier Professor of African American Studies. He is a United Methodist minister and currently serves as the Superintendent of the Baltimore-Harford District in Central Maryland. He was previously the Executive Director of the Multi-Ethnic Center for Ministry of the United Methodist Church in Columbia, Maryland. Additionally, he is Professor of Practical and Systematic Theology at St. Mary's Seminary and University in Baltimore, Maryland, and is an adjunct professor at Wesley Theological Seminary in Washington, DC. Dr. Hunt has previously held faculty and administrative appointments at American University, Goucher College, McKendree College, and Africa University (Zimbabwe). He is a graduate of the University of Maryland (B.A. Economics), Troy State University (M.B.A.), Wesley Theological Seminary (M.Div.), and the Graduate Theological Foundation (D.Min. and Ph.D.). Additionally, he has completed postdoctoral studies at St. Mary's Seminary in Baltimore, MD, and the Center of Theological Inquiry at Princeton University. He is the author of several publications including, *And Yet the Melody Lingers: Essays, Sermons and Prayers on Religion and Race*, *Blessed are the Peacemakers: A Theological Analysis of the Thought of Howard Thurman and Martin Luther King, Jr.*, *Upon the Rock: A Model* *for Ministry with Black Families,* and *Building Hope: New Church Development in the African-American Community.*

Paul Kirbas is Paul Tillich Professor of Theology and Culture. He is minister of the Presbyterian Church USA, and holds the Master of Divinity and Doctor of Ministry Degrees from Columbia Seminary, and a Ph.D. in Theological Studies from the Graduate Theological Foundation. His Ph.D. studies have focused on the intersection of theology and biotechnology, in collaboration with John Kerr, past Warden of the Society of Ordained Scientists in the United Kingdom. Dr. Kirbas has held pastorates at two large congregations in Florida, and currently serves as the Senior Pastor of the First Presbyterian Church of Wheaton, IL. His current academic appointments include an adjunct professorship in Theology, Culture and Biblical Studies at Wheaton College. He has led many conferences around the country and has produced DVD curriculum courses that have been used in a variety of religious and educational settings. He lives with his wife Jennifer and two children in metropolitan Chicago. He is the author of *Navigating Through a Stipulated Freedom: Discovering a Guiding Biblical Compass For the Journey of Biotechnology.*

Andrew Linzey is Henry Bergh Professor of Animal Ethics. He is a member of the Faculty of Theology in the University of Oxford and Director of the Oxford Centre for Animal Ethics. He also held the world's first academic post in Theology and Animal Welfare at Mansfield College, Oxford, 1992-2000, and at Blackfriars Hall, Oxford, from 2000-2006. From 1987 to 1992, he was Director of Studies of the Centre for the Study of Theology in the University of Essex, England, and from 1992 to 1996, he was Special Professor in Theology at the University of Nottingham, England. In 1998, he was Visiting Professor at the Koret School of Veterinary Medicine at the Hebrew University of Jerusalem. He is currently Honorary

Professor at the University of Winchester, England, and Special Professor at Saint Xavier University, Chicago. Professor Linzey has written more than 180 articles, and authored or edited twenty books on theology and ethics, including: *Animal Theology*; *Animals on the Agenda: Questions about Animals for Theology and Ethics*; *Animal Gospel: Christian Faith as If Animals Mattered*; and *Animal Rights: A Historical Anthology*. He is also co-editor of the *Dictionary of Ethics, Theology and Society* published by Routledge in 1995. Professor Linzey has lectured and broadcast extensively in Europe and the United States. His books have been translated into Italian, Spanish, German, Chinese, Taiwanese, and Japanese. In 2001, he was awarded a D.D. (Doctor of Divinity) degree by the Archbishop of Canterbury in recognition of his "unique and massive pioneering work at a scholarly level in the area of the theology of creation with particular reference to the rights and welfare of God's sentient creatures."

James Michaels is Professor of Jewish Studies. Rabbi Michaels has had a distinguished career as a pulpit rabbi and health care chaplain with roots in the academic community. Born in Auburn, NY, he received his BA from Cornell University in 1968, and was ordained and received his MA from the Hebrew Union College-Jewish Institute of Religion in New York in 1974. Immediately after ordination, he pursued graduate education in Jewish history at Yeshiva University in New York, and then entered the pulpit rabbinate. Rabbi Michaels has served in pulpits in Whitestone, NY, Wilkes-Barre, PA, and Flint, MI; throughout those years, he also worked as a health care chaplain at Bronx Psychiatric Center and with the Veterans Administration. He received his Doctor of Ministry in pastoral counseling from the Graduate Theological Foundation in 2006, with a specialization in bereavement counseling. In 2003, Rabbi Michaels was appointed Director of Pastoral Care at the Hebrew Home of Greater Washington in

Rockville, MD. He became a board certified chaplain in 2005 and was certified as a CPE supervisor in 2007. He has published articles in various academic and professional journals, as well as in on-line publications. He is married to Dr. Karen Markowitz, D.Pharm.

John H. Morgan is President and Fellow of the Foundation where he is the Karl Mannheim Professor of the History and Philosophy of the Social Sciences. He also is the Sir Julian Huxley Professor of the History and Philosophy of Education at Cloverdale College. Dr. Morgan holds the Ph.D. from the Hartford Seminary Foundation, the D.Sc. from the London College of Applied Science, and the Psy.D. from Foundation House/Oxford where he is also a Fellow. He has held postdoctoral appointments at Harvard, Yale, and Princeton, and regularly teaches in the Summer Programme in Theology at the University of Oxford. He has also been a National Science Foundation Science Faculty Fellow at the University of Notre Dame. His most recent publications include *Naturally Good: A Behavioral History of Moral Development (from Charles Darwin to E.O. Wilson)*, published 2005; *In The Absence of God: Religious Humanism as Spiritual Journey (with special reference to Julian Huxley)*, published 2006; *Being Human: Perspectives on Meaning and Interpretation (Essays in Religion, Culture and Personality)*, 2nd edition published 2006, and *In the Beginning: The Paleolithic Origins of Religious Consciousness*, published 2007. Forthcoming books for 2008 include *The New Paradigm in Ministry Education: A Radical Philosophy of Collaboration* and *The Gathering Storm: Accreditation and the Search for Accountability in American Higher Education*, both published by The Victoria Press.

Bernard J. O'Connor is Fellow, Dean of Studies of Foundation House/Rome, and John Henry Cardinal Newman Professor of Theology and Ecclesial Mediation. He received his B.A. in history/philosophy from St. Francis Xavier University, Nova Scotia; his

M.A. (Spirituality) from Creighton University; the M.Div/S.T.B. from St. Paul's University in Ottawa; the M.C.L./J.C.L. (Canon Law) from the University of Ottawa and S.T.L. and S.T.D. (Systematics) from the Gregorian University. Fr. Bernie, a native of Nova Scotia, was ordained in 1977 for that province's Diocese of Antigonish. In 1994 he received the J.D. from the University of Tennessee. A J.C.D. (with emphasis on international diplomacy) from the University of St. Thomas Aquinas, Rome, is pending. His numerous certifications and awards over the past 20 years include an Advanced Negotiation Certificate from Harvard Law School and certificates in international diplomacy and conflict management from the U.S. State Department at the Foreign Service Institute and from the UN Institute for Training and Research. He has twice been named Michigan Professor of the Year by the Carnegie/CASE Foundation. Between 1994 and 2004, Fr. Bernie was Assistant Dean at Eastern Michigan University and Visiting Professor for the Straus Institute at Pepperdine Law School and for Ave Maria College and Law School. He has been designated a "national expert in Constitutional philosophy" by the We The People Program in civic education; served on the State of Michigan Board of Ethics and was appointed to the U.S. Army National Committee on ROTC Education. In 1999, Fr. Bernie received the degree of Doctor of Humane Letters (honoris causa) from the Foundation. In 2004, Father Bernie was called to the Vatican to serve the Congregation of Eastern Churches. In 2005, he was appointed Chairperson of the Graduate Theological Foundation's Advisory Committee on Academic Development in Tribunal Studies.

Antonio Ramírez de León is Fellow and Bartolomé de Las Casas Professor of Hispanic Ministries and Catholic Studies. The recipient of the César Chávez Scholarship in Hispanic Ministries at the Foundation while working on his Master of Theology, Dr. Ramírez holds the Doctor of Philosophy in counseling from Saint

Mary's University in Texas, the Master of Arts in educational psychology from the University of Texas, and the Bachelor of Arts in psychology from the University of California. Dr. Ramírez has over 20 years of pastoral and missionary work experience in North, Central, and South America. He holds the Master of Theology from the Foundation where he is currently a candidate for the Doctor of Ministry.

Peter E. Roussakis is Charles Wesley Professor of Sacred Music. He holds B.S. and M.S. degrees from Southern Connecticut State University, the Master of Church Music from The Southern Baptist Theological Seminary, the D.Min. with an emphasis in Church Music from Austin Presbyterian Theological Seminary, taken cooperatively with the Royal School of Church Music, the Master of Sacred Theology in Liturgical Studies from Boston University, and the Ph.D. in Theological Studies from the Graduate Theological Foundation. Dr. Roussakis has taken further graduate studies at Harvard University and at Ashland Theological Seminary and Ohio University where he held faculty appointments. For a number of years at Southwestern University, in Georgetown, Texas, he held a professorship in sacred music. He was ordained in the Brethren Church. Earlier in his career, Dr. Roussakis served as a minister of music and for the past twenty years as a local pastor. He has authored numerous articles and several books, including *Classic Worships: With Brethren in Mind*, and *Confessing the Compendium: Praying the Lord's Prayer as Confessing Faith*. He wrote the introductions to two recently reprinted classic works in sacred music, Joseph Aston's *Music in Worship*, and J. Ernest Rattenbury's *The Evangelical Doctrines of Charles Wesley's Hymns*. His primary interests in sacred music include Anglican choral music literature and conducting, hymnology, and church music theology.

Vincent Strudwick is Fellow and Bishop John Tinsley Professor of Anglican Theology. He studied history at Nottingham University and theology at the monastic seminary at Kelham (both in U.K.) At Kelham he was later Vice Principal and lecturer in Church History. His research and teaching is specialized in the English Reformation and he has taught in several seminaries and universities both in the U.K. and the U.S. where he regularly teaches for the Smithsonian Institution. His final appointment in the U.K. was at Oxford University where he was Director of Theology Programmes in Continuing Education and Director of the University's International Summer Programme until 1999. After formal retirement, he still teaches for the Theology Faculty in Oxford where he functions regularly as Acting Chaplain at Corpus Christi College. In 1998, Canon Strudwick received the Doctor of Divinity honoris causa from the Foundation in recognition of his invaluable service in coordinating a relationship between this institution and Oxford University. He is an Emeritus Canon of Christ Church Cathedral in Oxford and Chamberlain and Honorary Fellow of Kellogg College, University of Oxford. His latest book is entitled Winter Change to Spring (2007).